Advanced Field
Procedures for
Emergencies

HUGH L. COFFEE
PALADIN PRESS · BOULDER, COLORADO

FOR KAREN

with a special thanks to Scott, and Frances, Ken, Pam, Dana, and John

Ditch Medicine: Advanced Field Procedures for Emergencies
by Hugh L.Coffee

Copyright © 1993 by Hugh L. Coffee

ISBN 0-87364-717-3
Printed in the United States of America

Published by Paladin Press, a division of
Paladin Enterprises, Inc., P.O. Box 1307,
Boulder, Colorado 80306, USA.
(303) 443-7250

Direct inquiries and/or orders to the above address.

Artwork by Gary Elliott and Denise Chung.

Contents

Warning

The techniques and procedures in this book are only to be administered by certified medical professionals. This book is not meant to be a substitute for proper and thorough education and training in the fields of medicine and emergency first aid.

The author, publisher, and distributors of this book disclaim any liability from any damages or injuries of any type that a reader or user of information contained in this book may encounter from the use or misuse of said information.

ACKNOWLEDGMENTS

The following medical professionals were of tremendous assistance, as the expertise represented by their various specialties contributed to the technical accuracy of the text.

Rose Akers, R.N. MSN
Steve Barnes, M.D.—Piedmont Orthopaedic Complex, Macon, Georgia
A. Scott Coffee, Pharm.D.
Glenn Dorner
Konrad Hell, Prof. Dr. Med.—Basel, Switzerland
Richard A. Knutson, M.D.—Delta Medical Center, Greenville, Mississippi
A.A. McMurray, Sr., M.D.

The photographs used in this book were contributed by the following individuals. Their photographs were indispensable, as they bring about a greater understanding of the narrative.

Rose Akers, R.N. MSN
C.V. Allmark—Tribal Refugee Welfare in Southeast Asia, Mirrabooka Western Australia
James Byron Dawson, M.D.—Deputy Director of the

Division of Forensic Science/The Georgia Bureau of
Investigation
Glenn Dorner
Shirley B. Fordham—Chief Forensic Photographer of the
Division of Forensic Science/The Georgia Bureau of
Investigation
Gerald T. Gowitt, M.D.—Chief Medical Examiner for Hall
and Henry Counties, Georgia
Richard A. Knutson, M.D.—Delta Medical Center,
Greenville, Mississippi
D.E. Rossey
Ronnie Stuart—Coroner, Henry County, Georgia
Hugh Wood—Australia

The gifted hands of Gary Elliott and Denise Chung produced artwork for this book when available photographs
would have failed to give the reader a complete understanding
of a topic.

Lynn Fulop and Kathy Shuman's methodical and profes-
sional arrangement of sentence format allowed the manuscript
to move from subject to subject in a clear, concise manner.

Scott Coffee (library research), John Cannon (subject of
many staged photographs), Karen Coffee (photographer),
Mike Mitchell (photographer and photographic development), Gary Elliott (artwork), and D.E. Rossey (military his-
torian) deserve special acknowledgment for their enthusiastic
and steadfast commitment to this project.

INTRODUCTION

From the days of the Roman Legionnaire with his short sword and pilum to the modern-day infantryman with his assault rifle and grenades, man's ability to tear the flesh and break the bones of his opponent has increased to new levels of grisly efficiency. Fortunately, for the soldier whose luck has run out and in the blink of an eye has been transformed from a combatant to a casualty, pre-hospital care of the injured has improved tremendously. Gone are the backward days when the field surgeon had more in common with an alchemist, protecting his "scientific secrets" of patient care from those who sought to understand the appropriateness of treating a gunshot wound with egg yolk, rose oil, and turpentine.

Along with technical advances in emergency medicine, patient care has entered new realms of delivery with the medical community's growing acceptance of medical paraprofessionals. Without these paraprofessionals at the "scene" to initiate advanced emergency medical procedures, many of the newest procedures in emergency medicine would be limited in their effectiveness because patient transport time would spoil their effects.

Modern weapons of war are found in the hands of combatants in the most remote regions. However, as a rule, mod-

1

ern military medicine, with its mobile hospitals and rapid patient evacuation to definitive health care, fails to follow combatants into the fields of conflict. It is in just such a scenario—where physicians are not to be found, patient transport to a hospital is measured in days instead of minutes, resources are limited, and the environment is hostile—that the Pre-Hospital Care Provider (PHCP) is in his element.

The subject matter in this book covers advanced medical procedures set in a field setting. Should the PHCP find himself on an isolated battlefield or in the middle of some form of civil disaster, his ability to employ the procedures covered in this book in a timely and competent manner will have a positive impact upon his patients.

For the wounded soldier who sees his strength ebbing into the warm pool of liquid by his side and seeks relief from his pain by crushing the blades of grass in his hands, thoughts are of family never to be seen again and aid from whatever quarter he can find it. Ditch medicine—the difference between life and death—often starts with the thud of a pair of boots landing beside the soldier and a PHCP simply grasping his patient's hand and peering into his ashen face.

S MALL WOUND REPAIR

For the Pre-Hospital Care Provider (PHCP), mastery of small wound repair techniques is of great importance in a field setting. From the laceration caused by an ax while chopping wood to an avulsion caused by an exploding mine, the ability to clean and close a wound properly can ensure quicker recovery of the patient with fewer associated complications. The traumatized site, if not treated early, can quickly develop into a life-endangering infection. Cosmetic distortion and reduced usage of the wound site can result from an open wound where tissues are left to heal with no proper surgical intervention (Photo 1). The PHCP can cause all three of these debilitating patient conditions to occur as a result of poor surgical practice.

The use of surgical tools and techniques used in small wound repair is not difficult to master. The basic manual skills—such as cutting, clamping, grasping, ligation, and tying—become second nature with a little practice.

CUTTING

Tissues are cut cleanly and perpendicular to their surfaces to promote healing. When skin is to be cut, it is first stretched taut, and the scalpel blade is held at a 90-degree angle to the

3

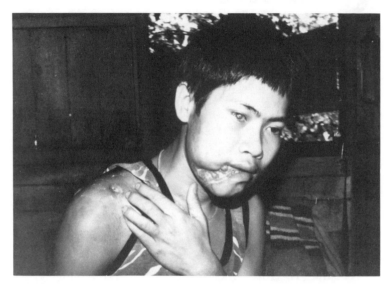

Photo 1: This 27-year-old Burmese patient was shot by soldiers through the right shoulder, striking the right cheek and fracturing the jawbone. The right eye was also injured. After five days of transport, he reached a dispensary. Due to a lack of medical resources, the wounds were allowed to heal as found. Even limited wound repair could have reduced the cosmetic distortion and possibly returned some function to the lower jaw. (Photo courtesy of Hugh Wood.)

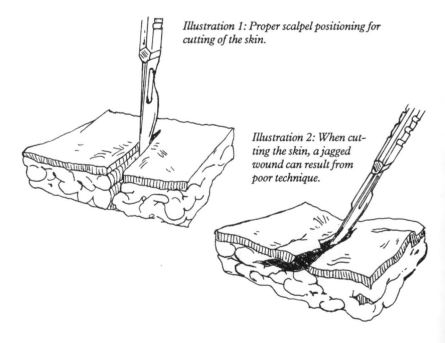

Illustration 1: Proper scalpel positioning for cutting of the skin.

Illustration 2: When cutting the skin, a jagged wound can result from poor technique.

surface of the skin to ensure a clean cut (Ill. 1). If the skin is held loosely or the PHCP hesitates, a jagged wound may result (Ill. 2). Cuts heal better if they are made parallel to wrinkle lines and across the lines of muscle pull (Ills. 3 and 4). For fine work and cutting of skin, the scalpel is the best tool (Ill. 5). When holding a #15 blade like an ink pen, the PHCP is ready for most cutting situations (Ill. 6).

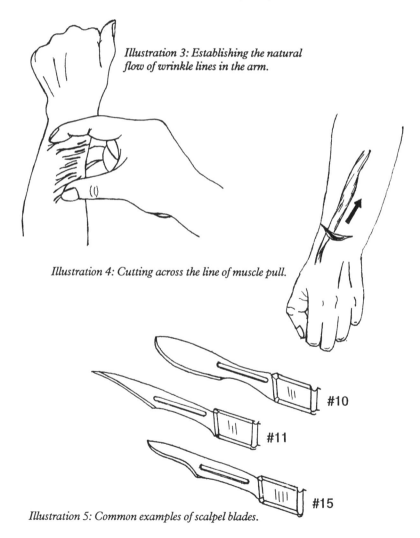

Illustration 3: Establishing the natural flow of wrinkle lines in the arm.

Illustration 4: Cutting across the line of muscle pull.

#10

#11

#15

Illustration 5: Common examples of scalpel blades.

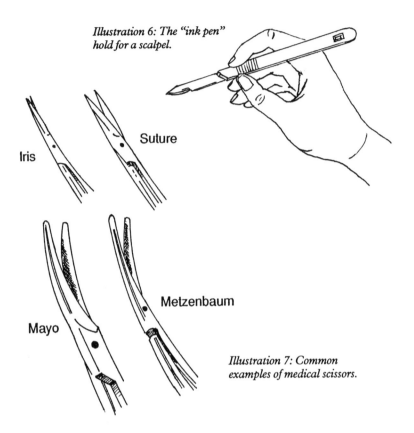

Illustration 6: The "ink pen" hold for a scalpel.

Iris

Suture

Mayo

Metzenbaum

Illustration 7: Common examples of medical scissors.

Scissors are used for cutting and dissecting the deeper tissues under the skin. Surgical scissors come in a variety of configurations. For the PHCP, the curved Metzenbaum and more heavily curved Mayo scissors will be satisfactory for most cutting needs. A small pair of iris and suture scissors are also useful (Ill. 7).

Blunt-pointed scissors are used when cutting in the wound. This reduces the accidental trauma of pointed blades stabbing surrounding tissue. The blunt points will allow the scissors to expose tissue by their spreading action.

Scissors cut by crushing. Therefore, dull scissors are dangerous, as they traumatize tissue.

CLAMPING

During suturing, it is important to visualize all aspects of the wound. This is difficult to do if the wound continually fills with blood. Clamping the vessel closed to stop hemorrhage into the wound is an easy way to maintain a dry field in which to work.

When clamping a vessel, the PHCP must be careful not to include surrounding tissue. Clamping crushes tissue and can also kill it, which may interfere with the healing of the wound. It is best to use the clamp with its concave side toward the tissue.

Clamps, as well as scissors, are best held with the thumb and ring finger pushed only partially into the rings of the instrument. The index finger is used to stabilize the instrument (Ills. 8 and 9).

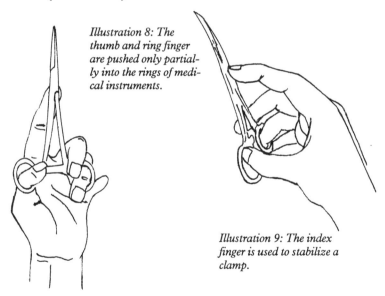

Illustration 8: The thumb and ring finger are pushed only partially into the rings of medical instruments.

Illustration 9: The index finger is used to stabilize a clamp.

GRASPING

Forceps are used for grasping. The fine-toothed Adson and the larger DeBakey allow the PHCP to hold tissue for exploration of the wound (Ills. 10 and 11).

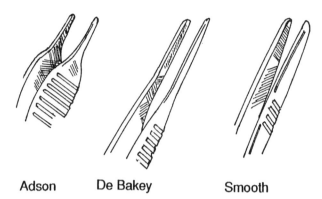

Adson   De Bakey   Smooth

Illustration 10: Commonly used forceps.

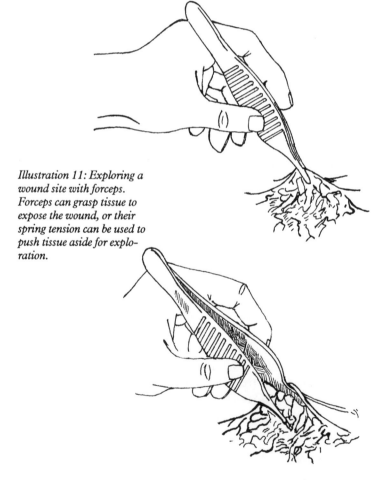

Illustration 11: Exploring a wound site with forceps. Forceps can grasp tissue to expose the wound, or their spring tension can be used to push tissue aside for exploration.

LIGATURE

Ligature is a critical technique for the PHCP who must stop life-endangering hemorrhage or needs a dry field in which to work. The bleeding artery or vein is first clamped. As the vessel is lifted and exposed, a fine absorbable suture (3-0 or 4-0) is tied below the clamp (Ill. 12). Once the PHCP has added an additional knot or two, the vessel is unclamped to check for leakage (Ill. 13).

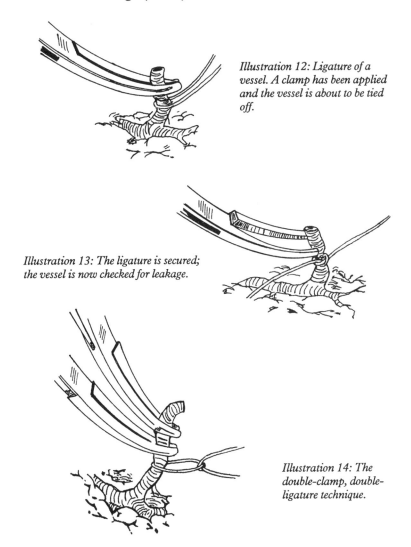

Illustration 12: Ligature of a vessel. A clamp has been applied and the vessel is about to be tied off.

Illustration 13: The ligature is secured; the vessel is now checked for leakage.

Illustration 14: The double-clamp, double-ligature technique.

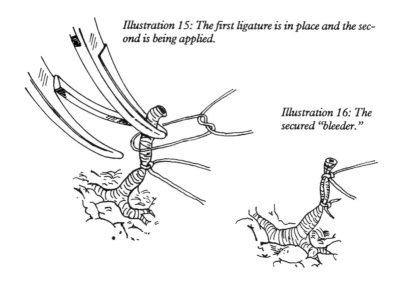

Illustration 15: The first ligature is in place and the second is being applied.

Illustration 16: The secured "bleeder."

With larger vessels or persistent bleeders, a double-clamp, double-ligature technique is used. Two clamps are applied, and the first ligature is applied under the lowest clamp (Ill. 14). Once this is secured, a second ligature is applied under the remaining clamp (Ill. 15). The last clamp is then removed to check for leakage (Ill. 16). When tightening the ligature, care should be taken not to cut the vessel in half.

TIES

There are several suture ties that would be applicable for PHCP usage. The instrument tie is probably the most useful because it helps conserve the length of the suture when several stitches are used (Ills. 17 through 26).

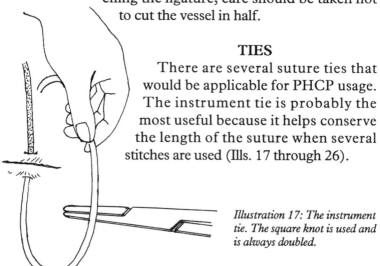

Illustration 17: The instrument tie. The square knot is used and is always doubled.

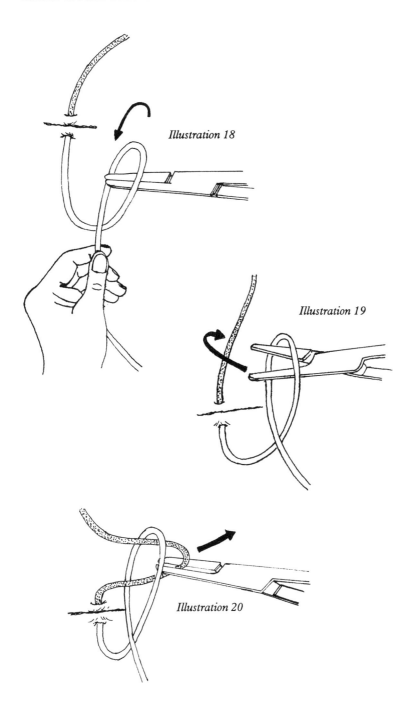

Illustration 18

Illustration 19

Illustration 20

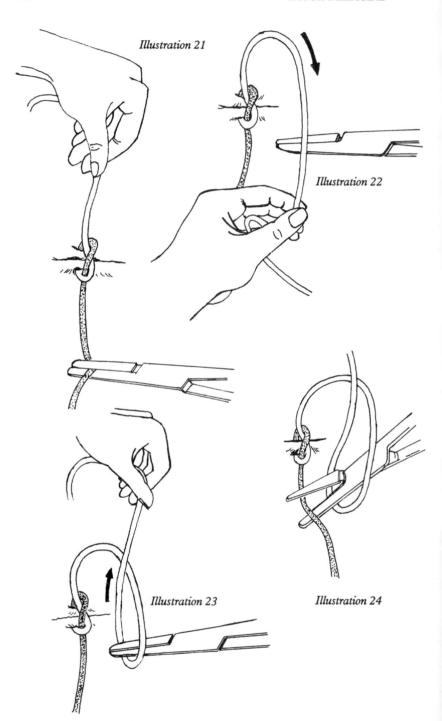

Illustration 21

Illustration 22

Illustration 23

Illustration 24

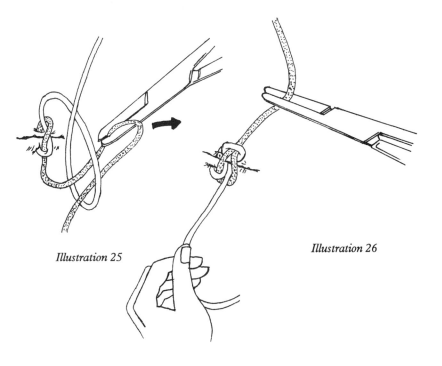

Illustration 25

Illustration 26

CLOSING THE WOUND

Suturing a wound closed is not simply a matter of "stitching" loose flesh together. For a wound to heal properly, attention must be given to the appropriate time to close a wound, debridement, mechanical cleansing, proper suture selection, and precise suture placement.

Timing for Wound Closure

Wound closure timing is categorized as primary closure, delayed primary closure, and healing by secondary intention (Ill. 27).

Primary closure of an open wound is the direct suturing of a clean wound in which there is no significant concern for infection. Primary closure is generally indicated if the wound has been satisfactorily debrided and mechanically cleaned, and it is less than 6 hours old. [1]

In delayed primary closure, the wound is 6 to 12 hours

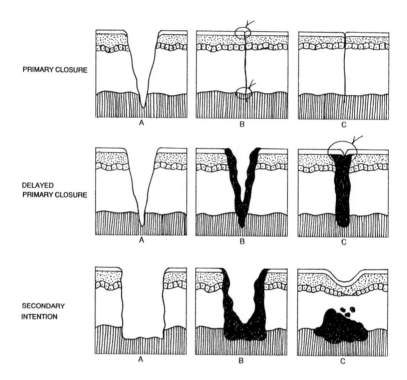

Illustration 27: Adapted from work found in Wound Care (Butterworth-Heinemann Limited, U.K., 1986, pg. 33) by Stephen Westaby.
Primary closure—Direct suturing of a wound that is less than 6 hours old.
Delayed primary closure—The wound is first seen 6 to 12 hours after injury. It is left open and closed in 3 to 5 days.
Healing by secondary intention—The wound is first seen 12 hours after injury. It is left open and closes by contraction and epithelisation.

old, which allows significant bacterial growth in the wound. The wound is left open and loosely packed with dressings. In 3 to 5 days, the wound will develop enough resistance to infection that closing it should not lead to complications (Ill. 28). [2] During World War I, it became common practice for Allied surgeons to treat ballistic wounds with debridement, wound excision, and delayed primary closure at 3 to 5 days after primary surgery (Ills. 29 through 33). [3]

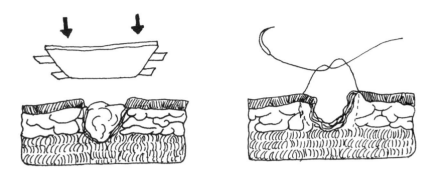

Illustration 28: Delayed primary closure of a wound. The wound is packed loosely and then closed in 3 to 5 days.

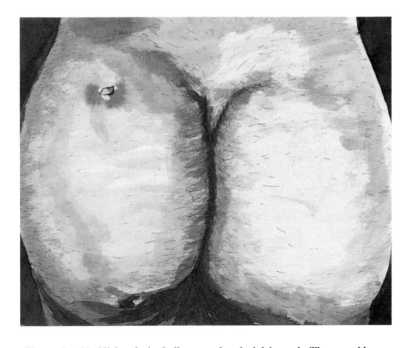

Illustration 29: High-velocity bullet wound to the left buttock. The wound has left small entry and exit holes. The underlying damaged muscle tissue along the bullet path has now become susceptible to gangrene. The entry and exit wounds as well as the anticipated line of incision are cleaned, shaved, and dried, and an antiseptic is applied.

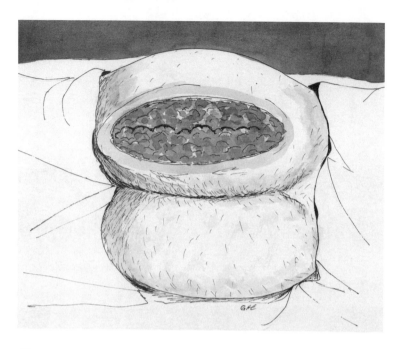

Illustration 30: To remove the dead and damaged muscle tissue, the buttock has been incised along and down to the depth of the bullet path. All nonvisible muscle tissue is now debrided and the open wound cleaned thoroughly.

Illustration 31: The wound is covered with dry, bulked dressing. It is not packed tightly, as this will restrict the flow of bacterial-laden inflammatory exudate.

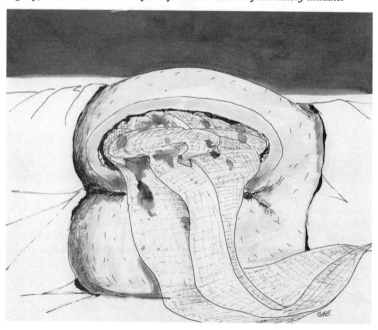

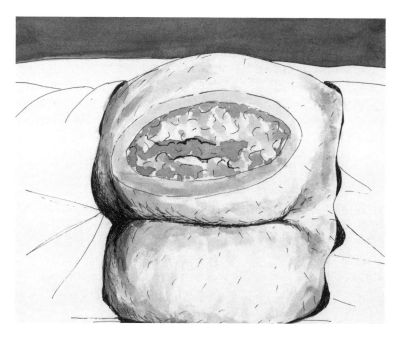

Illustration 32: With the wound left open and given proper dressing care, swelling and drainage will begin to disappear. The muscle tissue will take on a more normal color, and the wound site should be free of infection.

Illustration 33: Delayed primary closure of the wound after 3 to 5 days.

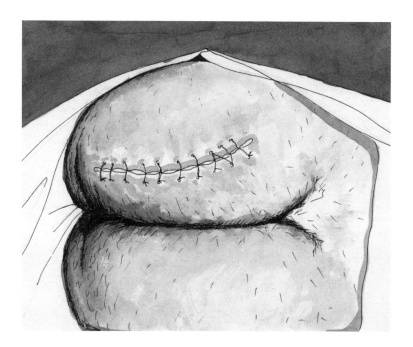

Healing by secondary intention is called for in wounds over 12 hours old. [4] The wound is left open and allowed to close itself by contraction and epithelization. This approach to wound care is indicated for the heavily contaminated wound with tissue loss and established infection. Wounds of this nature often require skin grafts at a later date by a skilled surgeon.

It must be remembered that even if a wound is not to be closed immediately, it should still be debrided and cleansed completely to promote proper healing. An infected wound is always a contraindication to wound closure, regardless of the length of time since the wound was inflicted. Further intervening factors that determine whether wound closure is appropriate are the health of surrounding tissue, general health of the patient, and degree of satisfactory blood supply to the affected area.

Debridement

When the decision has been made to suture a wound closed, a procedure for

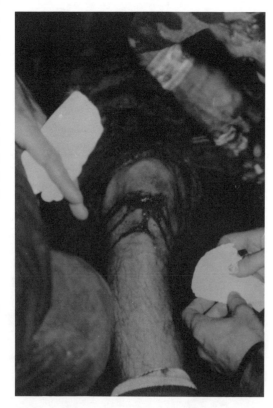

Photo 2: Laceration and abrasion to the right knee as a result of a fall upon rocks. Even minor wounds such as this one, if not debrided and cleaned properly, can quickly incapacitate a soldier due to infection. (Photo courtesy of D.E. Rossey.)

converting a contaminated wound to a clean one must be implemented first. Debridement of a wound, along with mechanical cleansing, is the most important step in decontaminating a traumatic wound (Photo 2).

Debridement has two main goals: 1) to remove tissue con-

Photos 3 and 4: This PHCP is using a surgical probe to locate the position of a 5.56mm bullet fragment. Small syringe needles (e.g., 25 gauge) can also be used. The needles are inserted through the skin at different angles until the foreign body is located. If this fragment had been left in place, the wound would probably have abcessed. (Photos courtesy of D.E. Rossey.)

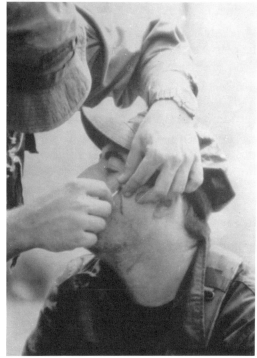

taminated by bacteria and foreign bodies (Photos 3 and 4), and 2) to remove permanently devitalized tissue (see Photo 20 in Chapter 2).

The dead or dying skin, muscle, and fat that is left in the wound act as a culture medium for both aerobic and anaerobic organisms. These devitalized structures quickly become infected and also inhibit the body's ability to fight infection by hindering the movement of white cells. The traumatized wound should be debrided as soon as possible to prevent the establishment of infection and its spread to healthy tissue. Antibiotics are not a replacement for debridement but an adjunct to it.

Determining what tissue should be debrided is based upon identifying the demarcation between compromised and healthy tissue. Guidelines in determining tissue viability are color, consistency, and the ability to bleed. Viable tissue will be reddish in color, firm in consistency, and fed with an adequate blood supply. Healthy muscle will contract when stimulated by a cutting blade.

Skin is generally more resistant to infection than other tissues due to its good blood supply. This allows the PHCP to be conservative in the debridement of skin. The debridement oftentimes can be restricted to only a narrow margin on the edges of the wound.

Unlike skin, muscle must be removed more aggressively. Dead muscle is a perfect medium for the development of gas gangrene. Any discolored, bruised, or noncontractile muscle must be excised totally, and all pockets must be laid open so the wound is saucered and able to drain freely.

Specialized tissue, such as nerves and tendons, presents a special problem because these structures do not have the degree of regenerative power that other structures have. When these structures become contaminated, high-pressure irrigation followed by removal of fragments that are not viable is the best course of action.

The procedure of debridement is usually best carried out with a scalpel. A scalpel gives precision and avoids a crushing action if scissors become dull. Effective debridement is dependent upon exposure of the wound, so incisions made at either end by the PHCP may be necessary to explore into deep wounds. Repetitive saline irrigation and sponging are also integral parts in the debridement process because irrigation loosens and flushes away contaminants while keeping tissues moist.

Mechanical Cleansing of the Wound

In conjunction with debridement, mechanical cleansing of the wound is necessary to ensure proper asepsis. Mechanical cleansing is a simple procedure of using hydraulic force and scrubbing the wound with an antiseptic solution in order to physically remove contaminants and destroy microorganisms.

Joseph Lister, a surgeon who lived in Glasgow during the 1800s, is credited with discovering antiseptic surgery. [5] His use of chemicals to kill bacteria was a cornerstone in his work, and some feel that his selection of the antiseptic phenol resulted from its use in deodorizing the putrefying sewers of his time. Today, a mild solution of Betadine is the antiseptic of choice for cleaning a wound. When Betadine is used, the PHCP needs to be attentive to the patient who is allergic to iodophor products. Also, high concentrations of Betadine can be toxic to healthy tissue and retard healing. Phisohex is effective when Betadine is not available or cannot be used.

When the PHCP begins cleaning the wound, it is best to wear a pair of sterile gloves, which are discarded and replaced with a new pair once the wound is ready for suturing. Aggressive scrubbing is important, as is high-pressure irrigation in traumatic wounds (a large syringe can be used in the field for high-pressure irrigation). However, care must be taken not to further traumatize wounded tissue or surrounding healthy tissue.

Once the wound site has been cleaned, draping the wound for suturing is of particular importance in the field. Draping decreases the chance of infection by providing a sterile barrier (field) in which to work. Without a surgical drape over the wound, the ends of suture would drag through contaminated areas and the PHCP's sterile gloves would quickly become dirty from contact with surrounding tissue. Commercial drapes are available that are disposable and have precut holes. Sterile towels work just as well when clamped together on the corners (see Photo 7).

Suture Selection

Suture is broadly classified as either absorbable or nonabsorbable. Absorbable suture is used to close muscle and subcutaneous tissue and to ligate blood vessels. Absorbable suture is broken down over time by the body and therefore is useful for tissues that lie deep and cannot be reached later in order to remove the suture. Catgut is the old traditional absorbable suture; however, synthetic sutures such as Dexon and Vicryl are preferred by many due to their more predictable rate of breakdown, greater tensile strength, and decreased tendency to cause inflammation.

Suggested Suture Size Usage For Related Anatomical Areas

	Skin	Subcutaneous tissue and muscle
Face	6-0 nylon	4-0, 5-0 dexon, vicryl
Scalp	4-0 nylon	3-0, 4-0 dexon, vicryl
Trunk	4-0 nylon	3-0, 4-0 dexon, vicryl
Extremities	4-0 nylon	4-0 dexon, vicryl
Hands, feet	5-0, 4-0 nylon	5-0, 4-0 dexon, vicryl
Mucous membranes		5-0, 4-0 dexon, vicryl

Illustration 34: Adapted from work found in Emergency Medicine: A Comprehensive Review *(An Aspen Publication, Rockville, MD, 1983, p. 142) by Thomas Clarke Kravis and Carmen Germaine Warner. The chapter, written by Davis Cracroft, is titled "Minor Lacerations and Abrasions."*

Nonabsorbable sutures are used in the closure of skin and approximation of lacerated tendons. Multifilament (woven) nonabsorbable sutures, such as silk and cotton, are often left on the shelf because monofilament nonabsorbable nylon or polypropylene are usually chosen. The single strand of a monofilament suture does not provide places for bacteria to hide (as does multifilament suture) and is therefore used when the possibility of infection is high. The main drawback of monofilament suture is that it does not handle as well or hold its knot as well as multifilament suture.

Sutures range in size from the very large #5 to the barely visible 12-0 filaments. Suggested suture size for body locations is given in Illustration 34.

Precise Suture Placement

Once it has been determined that the timing is appropriate for closure and the wound has been prepared properly (cleaned, debrided, and anesthetized), attention turns to precise suture placement (Ills. 35 through 38).

Illustration 35: Closing the wound. A) Mechanical cleansing.

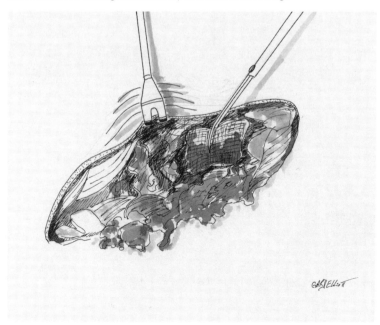

Illustration 36: B) Irrigation.

Illustration 37: C) Debridement.

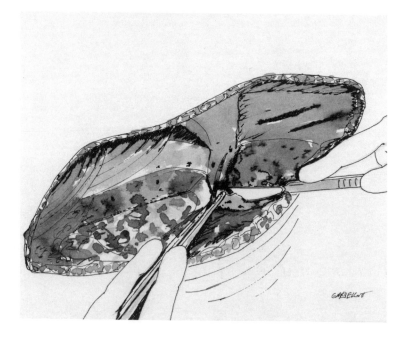

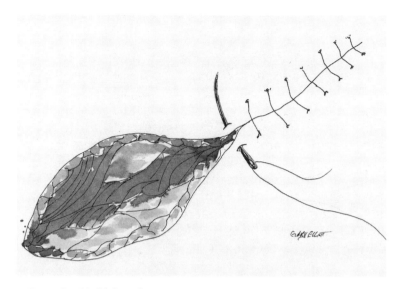

Illustration 38: D) Suturing.

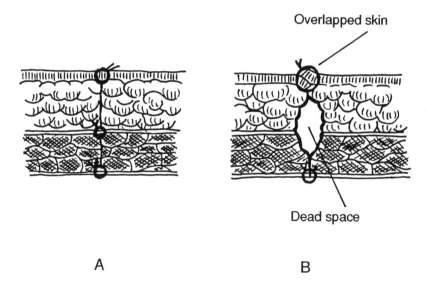

A   B

Illustration 39: A) Correct alignment of wound layers. The two deepest sutures should be absorbable. B) Suture being drawn too tight has resulted in overlapped skin. Failure to place a suture has resulted in dead space.

A wound is sutured closed to obliterate space, stop hemorrhage, and provide physical strength to the separated tissue
surfaces during the healing process. Special care must be
taken to align the various layers of the wound in close apposi-
tion (mucosa to mucosa, muscle to muscle, and skin to skin)
so that a minimal amount of new connective tissue will be
required to restore structural integrity as well as to prevent the
creation of dead spaces and overlapped skin (Ill. 39). If dead
spaces are left, they will fill with serum or blood, which will
provide a fertile ground for infection. Jagged wound edges
must be "trimmed up" to remove devitalized tissue and
ensure proper tissue alignment (Ill. 40).

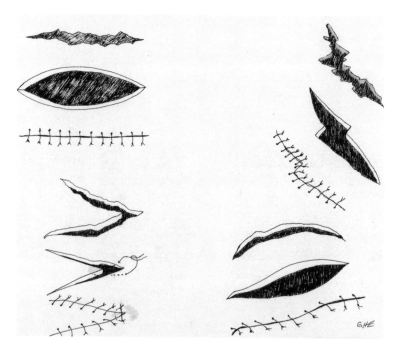

Illustration 40: Adapted from work found in Emergency Medicine: A
Comprehensive Review *(An Aspen Publication, Rockville, MD, 1983, p. 149)
by Thomas Clarke Kravis and Carmen Germaine Warner. The chapter, written by Davis Cracroft, is titled "Minor Lacerations and Abrasions."*

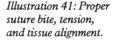

Illustration 41: Proper suture bite, tension, and tissue alignment.

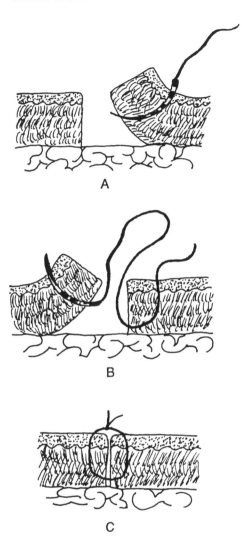

A

B

C

Particular attention must be given to the tightness of the suture tie, the size of the tissue "bite," and the distance between sutures. The suture tension should be just enough to approximate the edges (Ill. 41). When the suture is tied too tight, the wound edges are inverted, making the suture line fine in appearance, but rolled-under edges will heal weakly by secondary intention (Ill. 42).

A "bite" of tissue that is too close to the edge

Illustration 42: Suture tied too tightly, resulting in rolled-under edges.

may tear out, whereas a bite that is too wide can make alignment of the edges difficult. Too many sutures can lead to tissue strangulation. Conversely, too few can result in tissue edges that are not brought close to each other throughout the wound (Ill. 43).

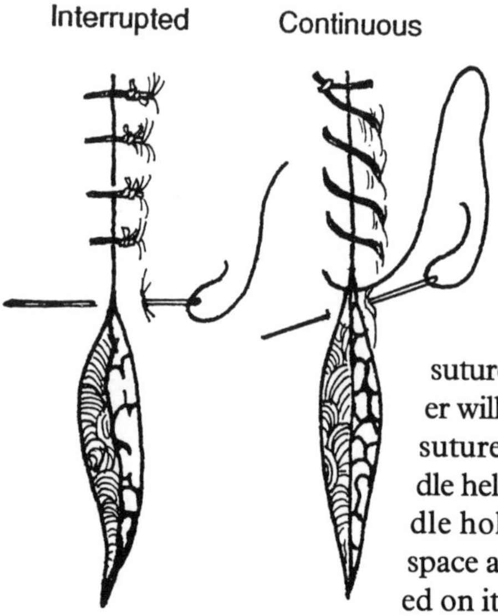

Interrupted   Continuous

Illustration 43: Proper suture spacing. The interrupted suture closure is the standard for wound closure. The continuous running closure can be threaded rapidly and thus is useful in emergency situations where numerous closures have to be made quickly.

Proper positioning of the suture needle in the needle holder will assist the PHCP in correct suture placement. A suture needle held perpendicular to the needle holder works well in limited space as the needle holder is rotated on its axis. It is the position for general-purpose work. Placing the plane of the needle curve parallel to the needle handle is useful in sewing layers parallel to the surface in deep wounds. Grasping the needle near the end (toward the suture) is suitable for soft tissue, as it allows maximum needle length to be inserted through the tissue. This action allows for reduced incidence of needle slippage. Grasping the needle near the point may be necessary if increased driving force is needed to pierce tough tissue.

The PHCP will develop an "eye" for the procedure that has as a goal a wound with a uniform wound line with no wrinkled tissue at the edges. For best results when closing the wound, the PHCP should remember the following:

1. Appose the various layers accurately.
2. Tie the suture with minimum tension.
3. Use the finest practical suture size.
4. Double the square knot.

Suture Removal

Correct timing for suture removal is dependent upon the patient's healing powers. If the patient's overall health is good, removal of the suture at the earliest appropriate time will help prevent the "railroad track" scarring associated with suture that has been left in place too long (usually past the fourteenth day of wound closure). If there is uncertainty as to whether the wound will hold up if the sutures are removed,

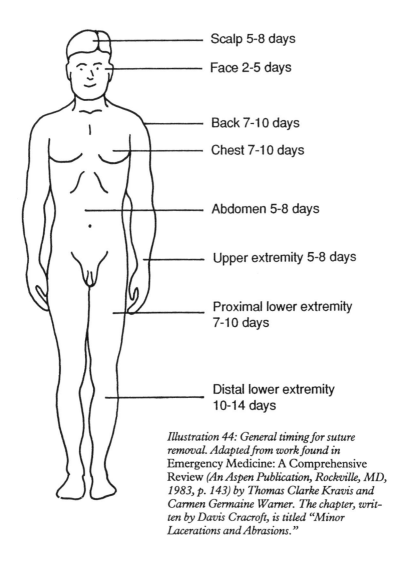

Scalp 5-8 days

Face 2-5 days

Back 7-10 days

Chest 7-10 days

Abdomen 5-8 days

Upper extremity 5-8 days

Proximal lower extremity 7-10 days

Distal lower extremity 10-14 days

Illustration 44: General timing for suture removal. Adapted from work found in Emergency Medicine: A Comprehensive Review *(An Aspen Publication, Rockville, MD, 1983, p. 143) by Thomas Clarke Kravis and Carmen Germaine Warner. The chapter, written by Davis Cracroft, is titled "Minor Lacerations and Abrasions."*

alternating sutures can be removed and the wound rechecked in a few days. A general guide for timing suture removal is given in Illustration 44.

When removing a suture, it may be necessary to lift it with forceps before cutting. The suture is cut close to the skin (see Photo 18). The goal of the technique is to prevent surface material from being dragged into the track once occupied by the suture (see Photo 19).

Wound Drains

The application of a wound drain is not usually a step in suturing a wound closed. The PHCP will be confronted with deep puncture and penetrating wounds, and for that reason he would be lacking in his patient care skills if he were not able to employ the use of a drain.

Wound drains are used to remove fluid or pus from cavities or abscesses. In the 1800s, the English surgeon Lawson Tait was quoted as saying, "When in doubt, drain." [6] Failure to use a drain to remove pus was considered negligent in his time, where in that preantibiotic period the drain was often life-saving.

Drains are most effective when placed in a deep wound with a narrow opening, which needs to heal from below first. But use of a drain is not hazard-free. Since it is a foreign body in an infected area, it can allow microorganisms to enter the wound. This can be compounded by dirty, moist, long-standing dressings.

One of the most commonly used drains is the Penrose (Photo 5). It is a pliable, flat rubber tube that varies in length. The Penrose drain is an overflow drain and as such should be placed as deep in the wound as possible. To secure the drain, it is sutured to the wound's edge and a safety pin placed in the exposed end to prevent it from slipping into the wound (Ill. 45). When the drain becomes clogged, it is generally better to simply replace it with a new one rather than try to open the obstructed drain.

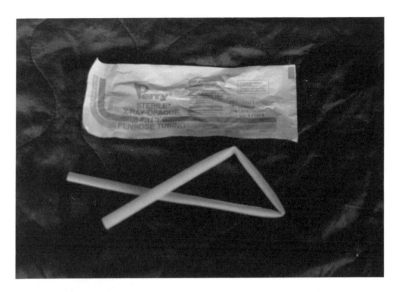

Photo 5: Penrose drain.

Illustration 45: Proper use of the Penrose drain. It has been placed deep in the wound and sutured to the wound edge, and it has a safety pin in place.

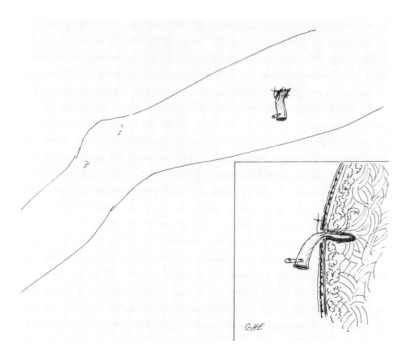

When drainage has stopped or slowed dramatically, the PHCP can consider removal of the drain. In determining whether or not to remove the drain, first loosen it and slowly advance it further into the wound cavity. If no further drainage is found deeper in the wound and the wound cavity has shrunk to just larger than the drain, it is probably appropriate to remove it.

A CASE STUDY

In the following series of photographs (Photos 6 through 19), a PHCP closes a laceration to the left thigh. The 34-year-old patient was in good health with no pertinent medical history (i.e., allergies). The wound was inflicted by a sharp blade. Efforts to close the wound were begun approximately 10 minutes after the laceration had occurred.

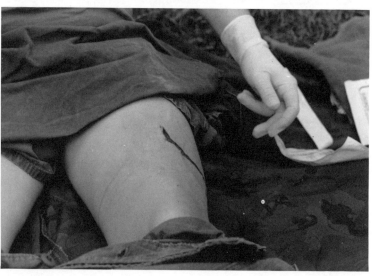

Photo 6: Laceration to the left thigh.

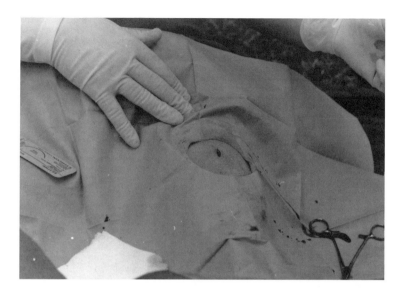

Photo 7: The wound has been cleaned with sterile water and Betadine. No debridement was needed due to a clean cut. The wound has been anesthetized with Lidocaine. The operating area is draped, providing the PHCP with a sterile area in which to work.

Photo 8: Suture being removed from its dispenser.

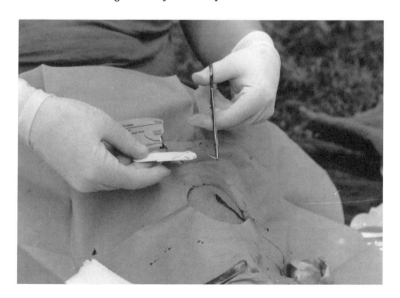

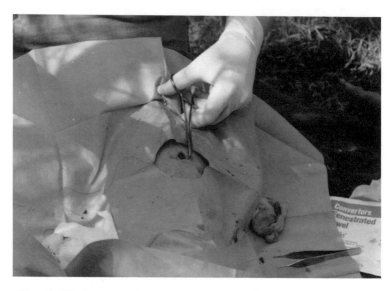

Photo 9: The first suture in place. Note how the needle is held in the needle holder.

Photo 10: The instrument tie.

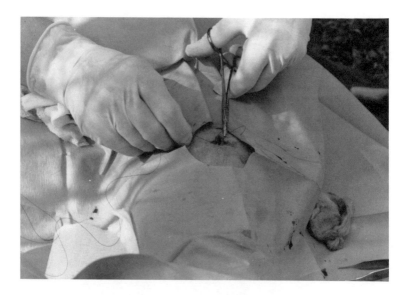

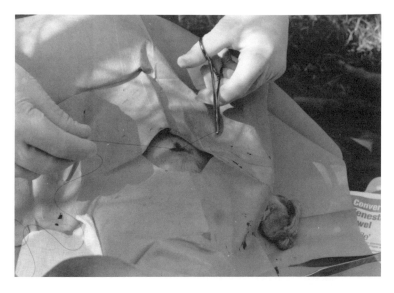

Photo 11: The square knot is doubled.

Photo 12: Cutting the suture end.

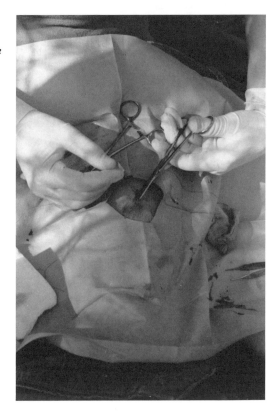

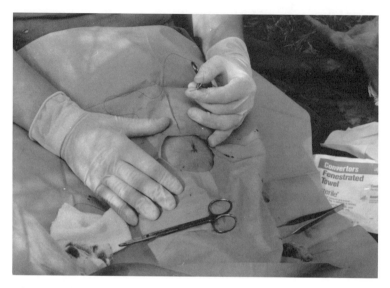

Photo 13: First suture in place. The wound has been cleaned up and is ready for the second suture.

Photo 14: Note use of palm hold and positioning of the needle holder close to the needle point. This is necessary in order to pierce the tough thigh skin. The PHCP is using his right thumb and index finger to locate the needle point, thus ensuring proper suture bite.

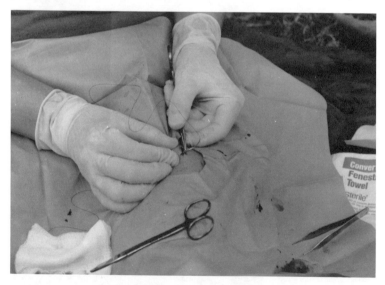

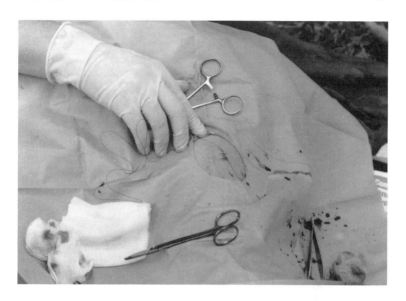

Photo 15: Second suture in place. The site is cleaned and ready for the final suture.

Photo 16: Final suture being threaded. Note proper suture bite.

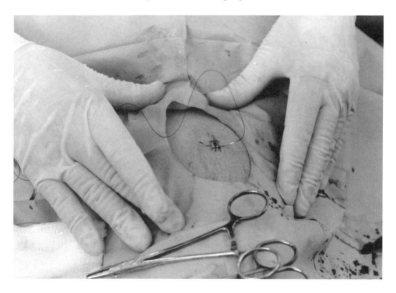

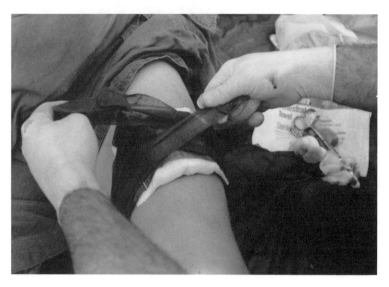

Photo 17: Neosporin ointment has been applied to the wound site and the wound is bandaged.

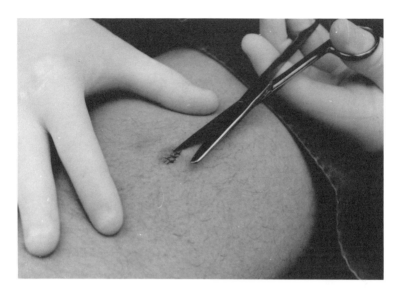

Photos 18 and 19: After 7 days, the sutures are being removed. The wound healed without complications and the scar was minimal.

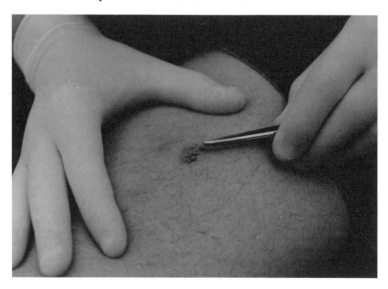

NOTES

[1] Thomas Clarke Kravis and Carmen Germaine Warner, *Emergency Medicine* (Rockville, MD: Aspen Systems Corporation, 1983), p. 138.

[2] Ibid. p. 138.

[3] G.J. Cooper and J.M. Ryan, "Interaction of penetrating missiles with tissues: Some common misapprehensions and implications for wound management," *British Journal of Surgery.* 1990, p. 609.

[4] Thomas Clarke Kravis and Carmen Germaine Warner, *Emergency Medicine* (Rockville, MD: Aspen Systems Corporation, 1983), p. 138.

[5] Warren H. Cole and Robert Elman, *Textbook of General Surgery* (New York, NY: Appleton-Century-Crofts, Inc., 1948), p. 24.

[6] Stephen Westaby, *Wound Care* (St. Louis, MO: The C.V. Mosby Company, 1986), p. 40.

CHAPTER 2

CARE FOR THE INFECTED WOUND

The first line of defense against infection is the unbroken skin. When the patient has suffered trauma to the body, this first line of defense is breached, thus allowing contaminating microorganisms to enter the wound. Once these microorganisms have contaminated the wound, they multiply exponentially, and, in twenty minutes, the number of Escherichia coli and Clostridium perfringens can double. [1]

There is no greater medium for the growth of microorganisms than the battlefield-inflicted wound or similar "dirty" wound (Photo 20). Battlefield and other traumatic wounds are characterized by dead or dying tissue, the presence of foreign matter, and contamination by bacteria, all leading to wound infection. Baron Jean Dominique Larrey, Napoleon's personal physician and surgeon, is said to have performed 200 amputations on the battlefield in a single day as the only recourse left for preventing infection. Predictably, more than 80 percent of these patients died anyway. [2]

ANTIBIOTIC THERAPY

Fortunately, advances in antibiotic therapy have reduced the need for amputations when the therapy is initiated in a timely manner. Around 1898, Friedrick established a param-

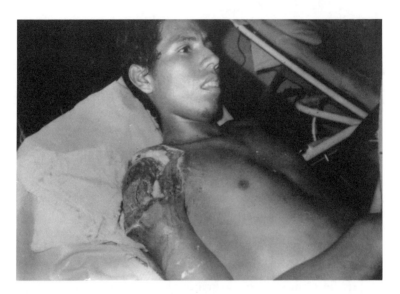

Photo 20: This FDN trooper received this battle wound to his shoulder from an AK-47 rifle while deep inside the Esteli region of Nicaragua. The wound was not immediately life-endangering, but there were no antibiotics to be given in the field, and evacuation to a hospital took 10 days. In this photograph, a physician has radically debrided the shoulder in an attempt to stop the spread of gangrene. The patient's arm was later removed in a last-ditch effort which failed to save this young soldier's life. (Photo courtesy of D.E. Rossey.)

eter of 6 hours from the time a wound is inflicted and contaminated to the occurrence of an invasive infection. [3] It is imperative for the PHCP to begin aggressive antibiotic therapy for the traumatized patient in order to avoid the consequences of an infected wound. The PHCP's guidelines for care should center around debridement and administration of antibiotics. Jacob and Setterstrom write:

> . . . surgical debridement and administration of antibiotics within as short a period of time as possible after wounding represents a crucial first step in the prevention of infection in open war injuries, factors which prolong the time of initial debridement can be expect-

ed to contribute to an increase in the incidence of wound infection. [4]

For the PHCP, quick administration of a broad-spectrum antibiotic (e.g., Ceftriaxone) to a patient who has suffered an open wound in the field is an appropriate initial response (Photo 21). Along this train of thought, Hell writes:

> Prompt administration of antibiotics is of the utmost importance in the treatment of wounds inflicted during a war or disaster. A single injection of a broad-spectrum drug with a long half-life should be given prophylactically to personnel on the battlefield to provide bactericidal coverage from the earliest possible moment after injury occurs. [5]

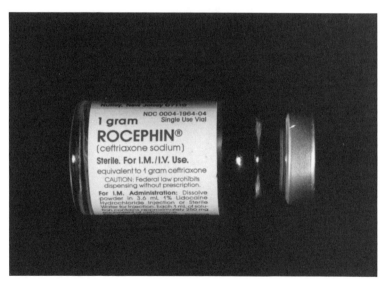

Photo 21: Vial of the broad-spectrum antibiotic Ceftriaxone. (Photo courtesy of Mike Mitchell.)

Once the patient has been stabilized and his wounds more closely evaluated, the PHCP should "target" if possible the specific types of bacteria that are commonly found in a par-

Wound Site	Diagnosis	Drug of Choice	Alternative Drugs
Muscle	Gas Gangrene	Penicillin G Potassium	Tetracycline Metronidazole Erythromycin Clindamycin
Bone	Osteomyelitis	Ciprofloxacin	Vancomycin
Abdomen	Peritonitis	Metronidazole	Cefoxitin Ampicillin
Skin	Burns	Vancomycin	Penicillin G Potassium
Skin	Trauma	Cefoxitin	Unasyn
Whole Body	Broad Range	Ceftriaxone	

Chart 1: Dosing of the drug of choice. (Source: Scott Coffee, Pharm.D.)

I.V. *	Oral *	I.M. *
0.5 million units every 6 hrs. in 50cc of D_5W over 30 mins.	250-500 mg every 6 hrs.	100,000 units per cc –Administer 5cc injection
400 mg every 12 hrs. over 1 hr. in 250cc D_5W	500 mg every 12 hrs.	
500 mg every 6 hrs. in 100cc of NS over 30 mins.	250-500 mg every 8 hrs.	
1 gram every 12 hrs. in 250cc of D_5W over 1 hr.		
1 gram every 8 hrs. in 100cc of D_5W over 30 mins.		Reconstitute 1 gram dose vial in 2cc of sterile H_2O –Administer 1 gram every 8 hrs.
1.0-2.0 grams every 12 hrs. in 100cc of D_5W over 30 mins. (No more than 4 grams in 24 hrs.)		Reconstitute 1 gram dose vial in 3.6cc of sterile H_2O –Administer 1 gram every 12 hrs.

* Dosings refer to drug of choice (column 3 on page 44).

ticular type of wound. This approach to antibiotic therapy is based on the premise that the PHCP will not have the benefit of laboratory confirmation of the offending microorganism. With this course of action, the PHCP stands the greatest chance of administering the most effective antibiotic to the microorganism most commonly associated with a certain wound (Chart 1). Given the aforementioned lack of laboratory facilities, the PHCP must be particularly careful in dosing the antibiotic since there will be no way to determine when the therapeutic blood levels have been reached.

Topical administration of antibiotics via powder, spray, or ointment should not be overlooked. The effectiveness of topical administration in conjunction with par-

enteral administration of antibiotics in combating development of local wound infection was proven in Vietnam, where
only 16 percent of the patients treated in this manner developed local wound infection. [6] Sulfamylon, Polybactrin, and
Neosporin are common topical antibiotics. The main short-
coming of topical administration is that it cannot reach bacteria located within the deeper portions of a wound. The PHCP
must depend upon parenteral administration of the antibiotic
to reach these deeply embedded microorganisms (Photo 22).

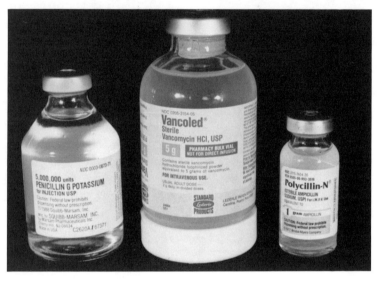

Photo 22: Common examples of IV-administered antibiotics. (Photo courtesy of Mike Mitchell.)

THE USE OF SUGAR TO ENHANCE WOUND HEALING

The use of antibiotics by the PHCP in the field has the
inherent dangers of improper dosing and allergic reactions.
The associated activities of preparing the IV/antibiotic infusion
and monitoring the IV drip rates can be difficult during patient
transport. Given these drawbacks, the use of granulated sugar
for the treatment of infected wounds offers a practical, proven

approach for wound care. The use of granulated sugar for treatment of infected wounds is recommended by some as a treatment of first choice. [7] Sugar has been called a nonspecific universal antimicrobial agent. [8] Based on its safety, ease of use, and availability, sugar therapy for the treatment of infected wounds is very applicable to the needs of the PHCP.

Sugar and honey were used to treat the wounds of combatants thousands of years ago. Battlefield wounds in ancient Egypt were treated with a mixture of honey and lard packed daily into the wound and covered with muslin. [9] Modern sugar therapy uses a combination of granulated sugar (sucrose) and povidone-iodine (PI) solution to enhance wound healing. [10]

As with any traumatic wound, the wound is first irrigated and debrided. Hemostasis is obtained prior to the application of the sugar/PI dressing since sugar can promote bleeding in a fresh wound. [11] A wait of 24 to 48 hours before the application of sugar is not unusual. [12] During this delay, a simple PI dressing is applied to the wound. Once bleeding is under control, deep wounds are treated by pouring granulated sugar into the wound, making sure to fill all cavities. The wound is then covered with a gauze sponge soaked in povidone-iodine solution. [13] Superficial wounds are dressed with PI-soaked gauze sponges coated with approximately 0.65 cm thickness of sugar. [14] (Photo 23)

In a few hours, the granulated sugar is dissolved into a "syrup" by body fluid drawn into the wound site. Since the effect of granulated sugar upon bacteria is based upon osmotic shock and withdrawal of water that is necessary for bacterial growth and reproduction, this diluted syrup has little antibacterial capacity and may aid rather than inhibit bacterial growth. [15] [16] So to continually inhibit bacterial growth, the wound is cleaned with water and repacked at least one to four times daily (or as soon as the granular sugar becomes diluted) with more solute (sugar) to "reconcentrate" the aqueous solution in the environment of the bacteria. [17]

A variety of case reports provide amazing data supporting

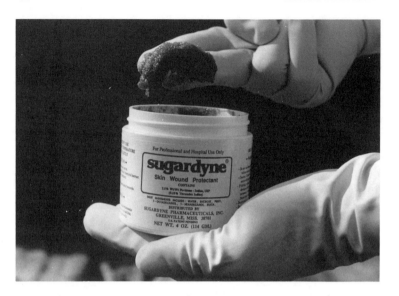

Photo 23: Sugardyne is a commercially available sugar/povidone-iodine compound. Its proven antimicrobial properties make it particularly useful for infected wounds encountered in the field. (Sugardyne donated by Dr. Richard A. Knutson; distributed by Sugardyne Pharmaceuticals, Inc., Greenville, MS 38701.)

the use of sugar in treating infected wounds. Dr. Leon Herszage treated 120 cases of infected wounds and other superficial lesions with ordinary granulated sugar purchased in a supermarket. [18] The sugar was not mixed with any antiseptic, and no antibiotics were used concurrently. Of these 120 cases, there was a 99.2 percent cure rate, with a time of cure varying between 9 days to 17 weeks. Odor and secretions from the wound usually diminished within 24 hours and disappeared in 72 to 96 hours from onset of treatment.

Like Dr. Herszage, Dr. Richard A. Knutson has had very successful results from the use of sugar in wounds. One of Dr. Knutson's most unique cases is recounted as follows.

A 93-year-old man was treated at Delta Medical Center for a fracture of his right hip. Concurrently, he received treatment for an old injury to his left leg, sustained 43 years earlier in

1936, when a tree had fallen on the leg while he was chopping wood. He had sustained an open fracture of the tibia and soft tissue loss to the leg anteriorly. Although the fracture had healed, bone remained exposed, surrounded by a chronic draining ulcer 20 cm x 8 cm overall. The patient was able to recall the various treatments used in attempts to heal the ulcer—iodoform, scarlet red, zinc oxide, nitrofurazone, sulfa, and a long list of antibiotics—all to no avail. He said that he had outlived six of the surgeons who had advised amputation. He was started on sugar/PI dressings, and then changed to treatment with sugar/PI compound as an inpatient. After hip surgery, the ulcer healed completely in 13 weeks. The ulcer defect filled completely, and skin grafting was not necessary. [19]

A CASE STUDY

A 19-year-old black man was treated for a shotgun blast to the right foot. The wound went completely through the foot, creating a 2.5 cm diameter hole on the dorsum of the foot and a 5 cm to 7.5 cm jagged wound on its plantar aspect. The wound was irrigated, debrided, and packed with iodoform. A similar procedure was done on his third hospital day. On day five and following, he was treated with whirlpool and sugar/PI compound and was ready for discharge, [having not taken] antibiotics in eight days. By seven weeks, the patient was nearly healed, with healing complete at nine weeks. He had minimal scarring with no requirements for skin grafting. (Photos 24 through 29) [20]

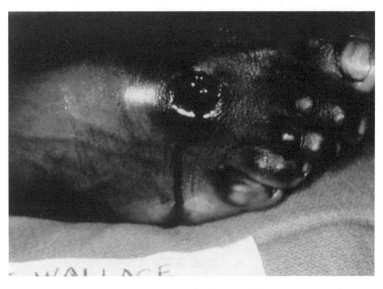

Photos 24 and 25: Entry (top of foot) and exit wounds from a 12-gauge shotgun blast to the right foot. (Photos courtesy of Dr. Richard A. Knutson.)

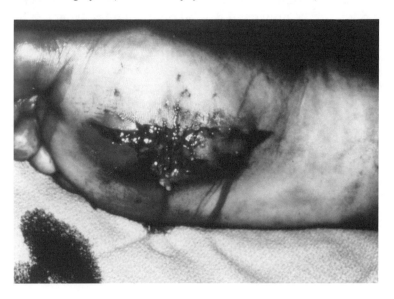

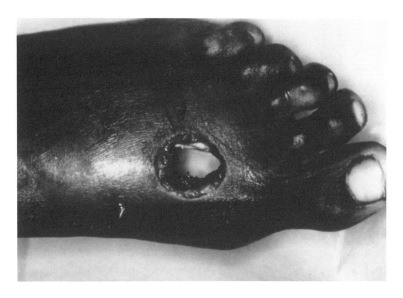

Photo 26: Wound as seen on day one after it was irrigated and debrided. Note careful and complete removal of all damaged tissue. (Photo courtesy of Dr. Richard A. Knutson.)

Photo 27: Wound as seen after two and a half weeks of healing. (Photo courtesy of Dr. Richard A. Knutson.)

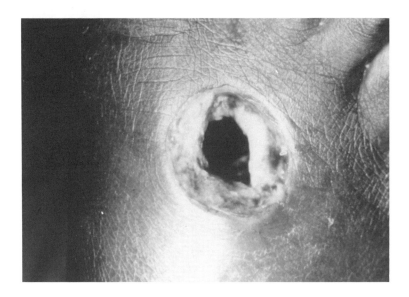

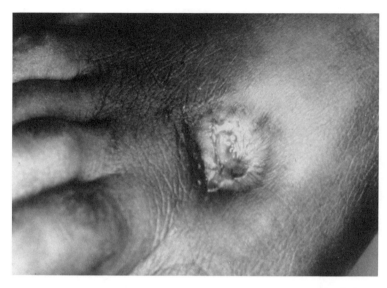

Photos 28 and 29: Healed wound at nine weeks. (Photo courtesy of Dr. Richard A. Knutson.)

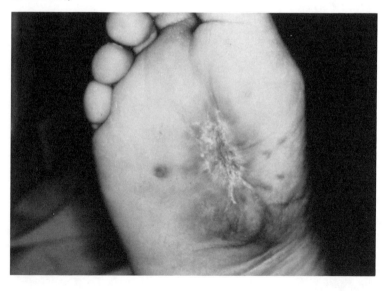

NOTES

[1] Konrad Hell, "Characteristics of the Ideal Antibiotic for Prevention of Wound Sepsis Among Military Forces in the Field," *Reviews of Infectious Diseases*, 1991, p. 165.

[2] Ibid. p. 164.

[3] Ibid. p. 165.

[4] Elliot Jacob and Jean Setterstrom, "Infection in War Wounds: Experience in Recent Military Conflicts and Future Considerations," *Military Medicine*, 1989, p. 313.

[5] Konrad Hell, "Characteristics of the Ideal Antibiotic for Prevention of Wound Sepsis Among Military Forces in the Field," *Reviews of Infectious Diseases*, 1991, p. 164.

[6] Elliot Jacob and Jean Setterstrom, "Infection in War Wounds: Experience in Recent Military Conflicts and Future Considerations," *Military Medicine*, 1989, p. 314.

[7] A.G. Tanner, E.R.T.C. Owen, and D.V. Seal, "Successful Treatment of Chronically Infected Wounds with Sugar Paste," *European Journal of Clinical Microbiology and Infectious Diseases*, 1988, p. 525.

[8] Jorge Chirife and Leon Herszage, "Sugar For Infected Wounds," *The Lancet*, 1982, p. 157.

[9] A.G. Tanner, E.R.T.C. Owen, and D.V. Seal, "Successful Treatment of Chronically Infected Wounds with Sugar Paste," *European Journal of Clinical Microbiology and Infectious Diseases*, 1988, p. 524.

[10] Richard A. Knutson, Lloyd A. Merbitz, Maurice A. Creekmore, and H. Gene Snipes, "Use of Sugar and Povidone-Iodine to Enhance Wound Healing: Five Years'

Experience," *Southern Medical Journal*, 1981, p. 1331.

[11] Tamas Szerafin, Miklos Vaszily, and Arpad Peterffy, "Granulated Sugar Treatment of Severe Mediastinitis After Open-Heart Surgery," *Scandinavian Journal of Thoracic Cardiovascular Surgery*, 1991, p. 77.

[12] Ibid. p. 77.

[13] Richard A. Knutson, Lloyd A. Merbitz, Maurice A. Creekmore, and H. Gene Snipes, "Use of Sugar and Povidone-Iodine to Enhance Wound Healing: Five Years' Experience," *Southern Medical Journal*, 1981, p. 1331.

[14] Ibid. p. 1331.

[15] Tamas Szerafin, Miklos Vaszily, and Arpad Peterffy, "Granulated Sugar Treatment of Severe Mediastinitis After Open-Heart Surgery," *Scandinavian Journal of Thoracic Cardiovascular Surgery*, 1991, p. 80.

[16] Jorge Chirife, Leon Herszage, Arabella Joseph, and Elisa S. Kohn, "In Vitro Study of Bacterial Growth Inhibition in Concentrated Sugar Solutions : Microbiological Basis for the Use of Sugar in Treating Infected Wounds," *Antimicrobial Agents and Chemotherapy*, 1983, p. 770.

[17] Richard A. Knutson, Lloyd A. Merbitz, Maurice A. Creekmore, and H. Gene Snipes, "Use of Sugar and Povidone-Iodine to Enhance Wound Healing: Five Years' Experience," *Southern Medical Journal*, 1981, p. 1332.

[18] Jorge Chirife, Leon Herszage, Arabella Joseph, and Elisa S. Kohn, "In Vitro Study of Bacterial Growth Inhibition in Concentrated Sugar Solutions: Microbiological Basis for the Use of Sugar in Treating Infected Wounds," *Antimicrobial Agents and Chemotherapy*, 1983, p. 766.

[19] Richard A. Knutson, Lloyd A. Merbitz, Maurice A. Creekmore, and H. Gene Snipes, "Use of Sugar and Povidone-Iodine to Enhance Wound Healing: Five Years' Experience," *Southern Medical Journal*, 1981, p. 1333.

[20] Ibid. pp. 1332 and 1333.

DECOMPRESSION AND DRAINAGE OF THE CHEST

The lung is elastic tissue that can accommodate temporary compression. Due to its elastic nature, the lung can sustain an amazing amount of trauma. Current literature on war-related chest wounds suggests that more than 85 percent of penetrating and perforating wounds of the chest can be managed with closed-tube thoracostomy. [1] The remaining percentage of wounds would necessitate the opening of the chest in order to surgically repair damaged structures that continue to hemorrhage or leak air.

Whether chest wounds are the result of blunt or penetrating trauma, they can lead to the life-endangering complications of tension pneumothorax, hemothorax, and hemopneumothorax. These types of developing complications require prompt intervention by relieving pressure in the tension pneumothorax or draining blood in the hemothorax. Without aggressive care, the patient's condition will deteriorate quickly as his respiratory and circulatory functions are compromised. Tension and hemothoraxsis are emergencies in which minutes count. In these instances, needle chest decompression and insertion of a chest tube in the field can make the life-or-death difference for a patient who has little hope for prompt transport to a hospital.

57

MECHANICS OF THE INJURY

The pleura is a thin layer of tissue that lines the inner side of the thoracic cavity as well as the lung itself. In the undamaged chest/lung, there is no space between the pleural layers because they ride close to one another. In the damaged chest/lung, air may flow between the two pleural layers, creating an unnatural space. As this space grows, it leads to a condition known as a pneumothorax. If bleeding is present, blood will accumulate between the two pleural linings, resulting in a hemothorax (Photo 30). When there is an escape of both air and blood into this "pleural space," a hemopneumothorax is present. A tension pneumothorax, which develops from either blunt or penetrating trauma to the lung, creates a one-way valve which allows air to enter the pleural space. The affected lung is soon collapsed, and the mediastinum is pushed in the opposite direction, resulting in impaired circulatory function and eventual impingement upon the remaining good lung (Ill. 46).

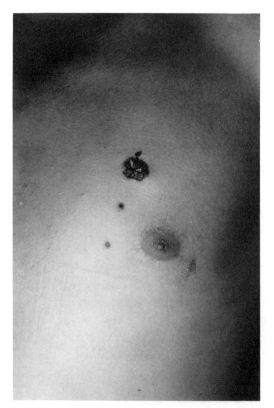

Photo 30: Gunshot wound to the chest. A wound of this type would result in a hemothorax. (Photo courtesy of the Georgia Bureau of Investigation/Photo Lab.)

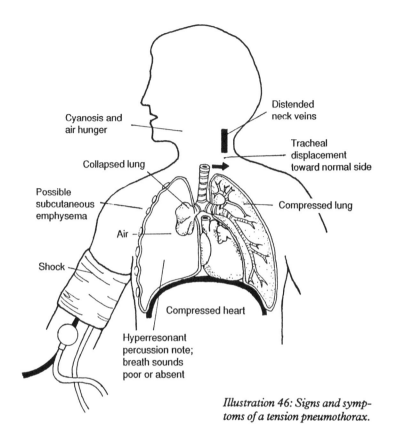

Cyanosis and air hunger

Distended neck veins

Tracheal displacement toward normal side

Collapsed lung

Possible subcutaneous emphysema

Compressed lung

Air

Shock

Compressed heart

Hyperresonant percussion note; breath sounds poor or absent

Illustration 46: Signs and symptoms of a tension pneumothorax.

A hemothorax develops as lacerated pulmonary vessels spill blood from the injured lung into the pleural space. The severity of a hemothorax is brought into greater clarity when one considers that each thoracic cavity may contain up to 3 liters of blood. [2] As blood fills the pleural space, the injured lung is soon displaced and collapsed. Circulation through the inferior and superior vena cavae, along with the respiratory functions of the uninjured lung, are eventually compromised by the growing pleural space. As more blood is lost into the pleural space, circulatory and respiratory functions deteriorate into a vicious cycle of shock and hypoxemia (Ill. 47).

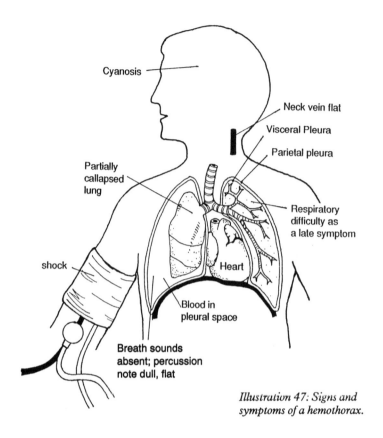

Cyanosis

Neck vein flat

Visceral Pleura

Parietal pleura

Partially callapsed lung

Respiratory difficulty as a late symptom

shock

Heart

Blood in pleural space

Breath sounds absent; percussion note dull, flat

Illustration 47: Signs and symptoms of a hemothorax.

NEEDLE CHEST DECOMPRESSION

An expedient technique for the relief of a tension pneu-mothorax is needle chest decompression. Needle chest decompression is a temporary measure requiring later replacement with a chest tube. When the patient exhibits signs and symptoms of a tension pneumothorax—with either marked respiratory distress, cyanosis, loss of consciousness, or loss of a radial pulse—a needle chest decompression is indicated. [3]

The procedure is begun by the PHCP identifying the fifth or sixth intercostal space in the midaxillary line on the injured side; an alternate site is the second intercostal space in the midclavicular line. [4] If a chest tube is on hand, it can be inserted in this second intercostal site in lieu of the needle. [5] After prepping the site with an antiseptic solution, a 14-gauge over-the-needle catheter (the same as used in IV therapy) is passed through a condom in order to make a one-way valve. The catheter is then inserted just over the top of the rib through the parietal pleura until air escapes. The needle is removed and the catheter is left in place until a chest tube can be inserted (Photo 31). After the procedure, the patient's torso should be elevated 20 to 30 degrees to assist in the movement of the trapped air.

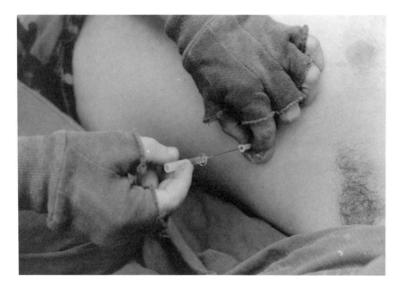

Photo 31: The PHCP is removing the needle while leaving the catheter in place through the condom. The condom will be unrolled to produce the one-way valve.

CHEST TUBE INSERTION

When chest trauma causes a symptomatic hemothorax, blood must be drained from the chest via a chest tube (Photo 32). Drainage of the hemorrhaged blood will have a positive effect on the patient's respiratory efforts, it will help avoid development of a constricting peel from the forming

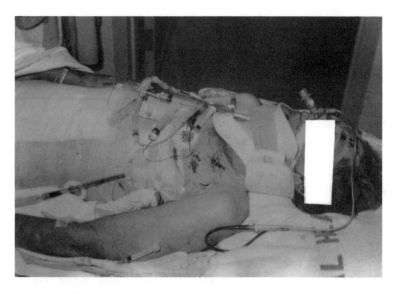

Photo 32: Chest tube in place on a patient who has suffered multiple trauma.
Also note endotracheal tube and nasogastric tube in place. (Photo courtesy of
Georgia Bureau of Investigation/Photo Lab.)

blood clot, and it also will allow measurement of the rate of
blood loss.

The two major considerations to be addressed prior to
insertion of the chest tube are adequate anesthesia of the
insertion site and proper tube placement. The procedure can
be extremely painful, so injection of the site with Lidocaine is
important. The diaphragm is often elevated on the side of the
injury, thus possible penetration of the liver or spleen could
occur if the chest tube is placed too low.

At the beginning of the procedure, the patient is placed on
his back with the arm of his injured side placed under his
head. A pillow is placed under his back to raise it slightly. The
sixth intercostal space on the mid-axillary line is prepped with
an antiseptic and the area is anesthetized. [6] The needle and
syringe used for the injection of the Lidocaine can also be
used to check tube placement by pushing it a little further into
the chest cavity and aspirating hemorrhaged blood. If blood is

not aspirated, the site is probably too low, and the PHCP is in danger of intra-abdominal placement of the chest tube.

Once the insertion site is verified, a 3 cm incision is made with a scalpel until fat is seen. The fat is spread by a clamp, exposing the intercostal muscles (Ill. 48). These muscles are also incised and spread open with a clamp, at which time blood and air should escape (Ill. 49).

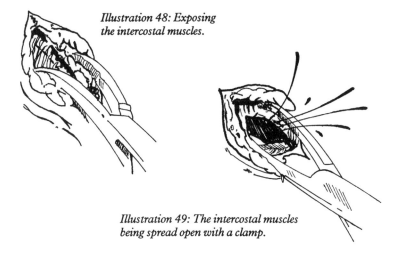

Illustration 48: Exposing the intercostal muscles.

Illustration 49: The intercostal muscles being spread open with a clamp.

The chest tube is pushed into the pleural cavity between the jaws of the clamp about 10 cm, or at least until the drainage holes on the tube are within the pleural space (Ill. 50). A Foley catheter can be used in a makeshift approach (Photo 33). Once the chest tube is in proper position, it is connected to tubing that leads to a drainage bottle. Proper tube placement can be evaluated by monitoring the rise and fall of the water in the drainage bottle with each inspiration and expiration. If water does not rise and fall, or if no bubbles are noted, tube placement should be reevaluated.

Illustration 50: Insertion of the chest tube.

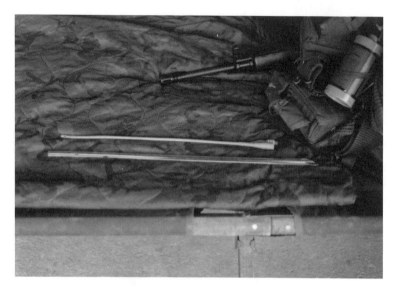

Photo 33: Chest tube in the foreground. Foley catheter in the background. Note drainage holes in the tubes that are placed inside the chest.

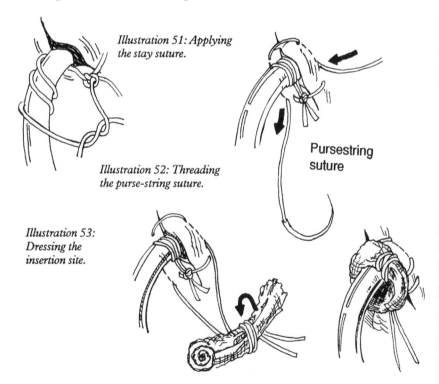

Illustration 51: Applying the stay suture.

Illustration 52: Threading the purse-string suture.

Pursestring suture

Illustration 53: Dressing the insertion site.

The chest tube is fastened to the outer chest wall with 3-0 size suture. To form an airtight seal, a stay suture is wrapped around the tube several times and drawn tight with another knot (Ill. 51). A purse-string suture is then threaded to ensure a seal when the chest tube is removed at a later date (Ill. 52). The extra suture from the purse string is wrapped around a 2 x 2 inch sponge and then wrapped around the tube to serve as a dressing (Ill. 53). The dressing is held down with tape.

THE DRAINAGE BOTTLE

The drainage bottle, which must lie below the patient in order to work, serves as a means to collect blood and fluids. More importantly, the drainage bottle and underwater seal take advantage of gravity as a means to effect drainage of the chest. Chest drainage is also assisted by exhalation, which pushes air and liquid out of the pleural space.

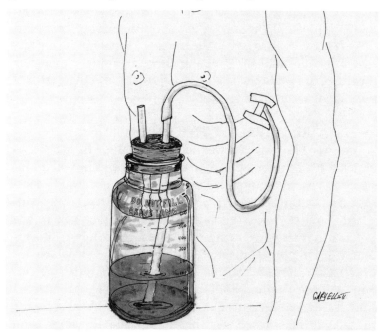

Illustration 54: Collection bottle and water seal.

For the water seal (one-way valve) to function properly, the end of the tubing must be below the surface of the sterile water. The drainage tube should be just a little under the surface of the water (Ill. 54). If the tube is too deep as a result of collection buildup, resistance to air passage through the tube can prevent air escape, resulting in a pneumothorax, even with a "functioning" chest drain. A 20- to 30-degree elevation of the patient's torso should help pool the blood and thereby facilitate drainage.

POST CHEST TUBE INSERTION ASSESSMENT

With fluid replacement and chest drainage, many pulmonary lacerations that do not directly involve a major vessel will heal on their own. Relief of the tension in the chest may be followed by hemorrhage from a vascular injury that can only be corrected by a surgeon opening the patient's chest to stop the bleeding. If drainage from the chest is less than 150 ml per hour, there are no large or continuous air leaks, and there is no major damage to the trachea, esophagus, bronchial tree, or cardiovascular system, drainage and other supportive measures are probably adequate. [7] This is particularly true if the patient's vital signs are stable.

REMOVAL OF THE CHEST TUBE

Once the lung has fully expanded and there have been no air leaks for 24 hours, the chest tube has been stopped up for 24 hours, or fluid output is less than 50 ml per day, the chest tube usually can be removed. [8]

An X-ray of the chest is taken to ensure that the lung is fully inflated (it is also used to check tube placement), but unfortunately this important diagnostic tool is not often available for the PHCP. The purse string is unrolled, stay sutures are cut, and, while the patient holds a deep breath, the chest tube is pulled free and the purse string closed (Ills. 55 and 56). A dressing is then placed over the incision site. It is not a good practice to remove the chest tube in the field, and, if at all possible, it should be left in until the patient has reached a hospital.

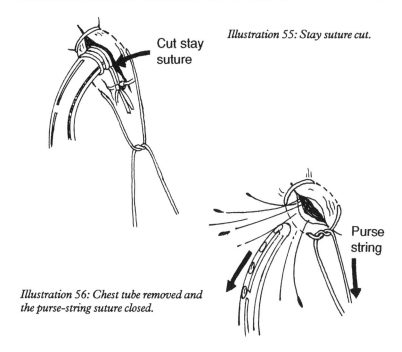

Cut stay suture

Illustration 55: Stay suture cut.

Purse string

Illustration 56: Chest tube removed and the purse-string suture closed.

COMPLICATIONS ASSOCIATED WITH NEEDLE CHEST DECOMPRESSION AND CHEST TUBE INSERTION

Needle chest decompression and chest tube insertion are not risk-free. Poor technique can easily contribute to the demise of the patient. Proper needle and tube placement, which will avoid lacerating the intercostal artery and vein that run around the inferior margin of each rib, is of particular concern. A needle or chest tube advanced too far into the chest can lacerate a variety of important structures. Poor patient assessment can lead to the creation of a pneumothorax by inappropriately initiating the procedures when they are not needed. And finally, during transport of the patient with a chest tube, it is not uncommon for the chest tube to be clamped off and removed from the water seal for ease of mobility. This practice should be avoided because the clamped-off tube can lead to a tension pneumothorax in the unhealed lung.

DRESSING THE CHEST WOUND

For needle chest decompression and chest tube drainage to function properly, the wound site (be it the result of a bullet or a knife) must be dressed with an occlusive dressing. The immediate application of an occlusive dressing along with other basic life-support procedures (i.e., oxygen and IV therapy) take initial precedence over needle chest decompression and chest tube drainage. The purpose of the occlusive dressing is to prevent air from entering the chest through the wound, with the possible consequence of a pneumothorax.

The dressing can consist of any material that will ensure an airtight seal over the wound (e.g., aluminum foil, plastic wrap, Vaseline gauze). The traditional technique is to tape down all four sides of the dressing (Ill. 57). The last edge is taped down after the patient exhales forcefully. The dressing should be large enough to cover at least 2 inches past the wound on all four sides. If tape won't stick to a wet or bloody chest, large trauma dressings can be held down with cravats that surround the chest. If an exit wound is present, as is commonly found with a gunshot wound, it must be covered too.

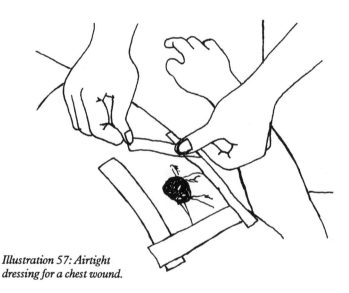

Illustration 57: Airtight dressing for a chest wound.

When the PHCP has neither the time nor equipment to carry out a needle chest decompression, a flutter valve dressing may be applied over the wound site to prevent the development of a tension pneumothorax. With the flutter valve, one corner of the occlusive dressing is left untaped (Ill. 58). As the patient inhales, the dressing will seal the wound. With exhalation, the free corner acts as a flutter valve to release air that is trapped in the chest. The advantage of the flutter valve over the traditional dressing approach is that the flutter valve does not tend to develop a tension pneumothorax that is sometimes seen with the traditional dressing approach.

On inspiration, air tight dressing
seals wounds, preventing air injury.

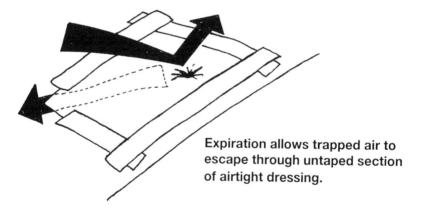

Expiration allows trapped air to
escape through untaped section
of airtight dressing.

Illustration 58: Flutter valve dressing for a chest wound.

Should a tension pneumothorax develop under a traditional dressing, one corner of the dressing is lifted up until the patient's condition improves. Once the patient's respiratory distress has abated, the wound is resealed. The procedure may have to be repeated a short time later. When a functional needle chest decompression or chest tube has been established, the flutter valve is taped closed.

NOTES

[1] Stephen Westaby, *Wound Care* (St. Louis, MO: The C.V. Mosby Company, 1986), p. 118.

[2] John Emory Campbell, *Basic Trauma Life Support* (Englewood Cliffs, NJ: Prentice-Hall, Inc., 1988), p. 97.

[3] Ibid. pp. 346-347.

[4] Ibid. p. 347.

[5] Thomas Clarke Kravis and Carmen Germaine Warner, *Emergency Medicine* (Rockville, MD: Aspen Systems Corporation, 1983), p. 1095.

[6] Ibid. p. 1097.

[7] Stephen Westaby, *Wound Care* (St. Louis, MO: The C.V. Mosby Company, 1986), p. 140.

[8] Walter J. Pories and Francis T. Thomas, *Office Surgery for Family Physicians* (Stoneham, MA: Butterworth Publishers, 1985), p. 163.

CHAPTER 4

INTRAVENOUS THERAPY

Intravenous therapy (IV), or parenteral therapy, refers to the route of administration of fluids and drugs by injection into the vascular system of the body. The first recorded injection into the veins of living animals occurred around the year 1658 when Sir Christopher Wren used a goose quill attached to a bladder to administer "medicaments" to a dog. [1] Since that time, the establishment of an IV has become recognized as a fundamental step in the care of a patient who has suffered from some form of trauma or medical emergency. The direct access to the body systems that the IV allows enhances the replenishment of lost body fluids and allows administered drugs to carry out their physiological actions faster than other means of drug administration. Establishment of an IV is not a difficult task, but it is one that should be thoroughly understood and skillfully executed in the field.

CLINICAL USE OF INTRAVENOUS THERAPY

In the hands of the PHCP, IV infusion gives the hemorrhagic body sufficient fluid to fill the "system," thus allowing the heart to operate efficiently until new blood is manufactured by the body or transfused from a donor. For the medical emergency, IV infusion provides a "lifeline" for the administration of drugs. IVs are started on patients for the following three general reasons:

1. replenishment of fluid in the circulatory system when there is a volume deficit due to hemorrhage, dehydration, burns, etc.

2. establishment of a secure access for drug administration in trauma and medically related emergencies

3. establishment of a means of intravenous administration prior to anticipated patient deterioration when accessing the vein at a later date would be difficult [2]

The Three Primary IV Solutions and Their Uses

D5W—Five percent dextrose in sterile water is given in cases where an IV is established as a lifeline or medication route.

NS—Normal Saline, which is 0.09 percent sodium chloride in sterile water, is used for irrigation, rehydration, and occasional burn cases.

RL—Ringer's Lactate is a solution of electrolytes that are isotonic with body composition. This solution is the IV fluid of choice for trauma cases. Although Ringer's Lactate does not have the red blood cells that carry oxygen, it can be used to replace up to two-thirds of the blood supply of a healthy individual before body functions start to fail. [3]

Selection of the IV Catheter and Drip Set

For trauma patients, volume replacement for the associated hemorrhage should be carried out with Ringer's Lactate. Two IV lines (in different sites) should be started with large-bore IV catheters in the range of 14 to 18 gauge. The appropriate drip set is the 10-drops-per-ml (10 drops/ml) macro-drip set, or, if available, the drip set for blood infusion can be used. This will allow rapid infusion of large volumes of Ringer's Lactate.

In cases of severe blood loss, pressure infusion and the 3 for 1 rule are appropriate. For pressure infusion of the IV fluid, a blood pressure cuff is wrapped around the IV bag and

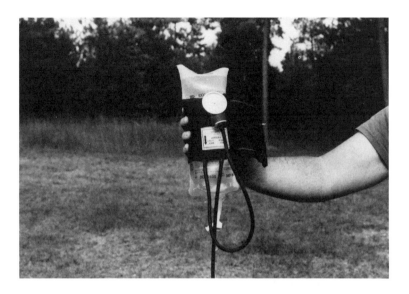

Photo 34: Use of a blood pressure cuff to pressure-infuse IV fluids.

Photo 35: This PHCP holds both a macrodip chamber (on left) and a microdip chamber (on right). Note the fine metal tube in the microdip chamber that allows for smaller droplets and thus greater regulation of fluid infusion.

inflated (Photo 34). This technique will infuse the IV fluid faster than it can be dripped in. In regard to the 3 for 1 rule, 3 ml of Ringer's Lactate should be given for each ml of blood loss. [4] For the administration of medications, D5W is the fluid of choice flowed through a 60-drops-per-ml (60 drops/ml) microdrip set (Photo 35). The microdrip set will give greater precision in administering a drug due to finer adjustment of the flow rate. Catheter size can range from 18 gauge to the smaller 20 gauge.

Potential Complications from IV Therapy

The chief complications that PHCPs must be attentive to when administering IV fluids are circulatory overload, speed shock, infiltration of the vein, and microbial contamination.

Circulatory overload can occur when a runaway IV infuses too much fluid. As the circulatory system is flooded, fluid is forced into the lungs, causing pulmonary edema. Circulatory overload can be prevented by observing the patient's vital signs and tapering back the flow rate until the patient's condition improves. A person suffering from circulatory overload will exhibit the following signs:

1. venous distention
2. rise in blood pressure
3. coughing
4. shortness of breath
5. increased lung edema
6. cyanosis

When a patient does begin to exhibit signs of circulatory overload, first elevate his head. Reduce the flow rate to just enough "to keep the vein open" (TKO). The IV should be left in place because in severe cases medication may need to be given to correct pulmonary edema.

When medications are given via the IV route, the PHCP should be attentive to speed shock. Speed shock results from a medication being administered too rapidly through the IV system. The patient suffering from speed shock will exhibit a flushed face, headache, loss of consciousness, shock, and pos-

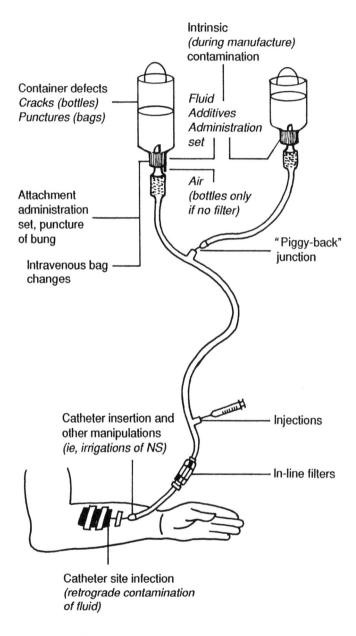

Illustration 59: Routes of intrinsic and extrinsic contamination.

sible cardiac arrest. If speed shock develops, administration of the drug is stopped. The IV is left in place, since this lifeline will be needed to administer countermeasures.

Infiltration is a common problem in the field, where the IV catheter is dislodged from the vein, spilling IV fluid into the surrounding tissue. Infiltration can cause tissue damage. The situation presents itself as a non- or poorly flowing IV with swelling of the skin as the IV fluid pools under it. When infiltration occurs, the IV catheter is removed, another site is selected, and the patient is "stuck" again.

The sources of microbial contamination during IV therapy are ubiquitous. The origin of the contamination is classified as either extrinsic or intrinsic. The PHCP must be particularly attuned to the likelihood of contamination as a result of the environment in which he must work. Intrinsic origin contamination, rare in modern processing procedures, results when microorganisms are introduced during the commercial manufacturing of the IV fluids. Extrinsic origin contamination results from poor aseptic procedures during IV administration (Ill. 59). Related septicemia is an avoidable patient complication. A common source of extrinsic origin contamination is skin flora on both the patient and PHCP. These microorganisms vary from staphylococcus epidermidis to gram-negative bacilli.

Another area of extrinsic origin contamination that the PHCP can control is auto-infection. IV catheters inserted in patients who have active infections in the body easily become contaminated with the same organisms that infected the primary site. These auto-infections are generally transmitted from the infected wound site to the IV site by the hands of the PHCP or the patient. Auto-infections can also result from microorganisms being transported to the IV insertion site via the bloodstream (Ill. 60).

It is a good practice to inspect the IV insertion site at least every 48 hours. If no problems are found, new antiseptic ointment and dressings are applied. It is best to discontinue use of an IV site after about 72 hours. Given the filthy conditions in

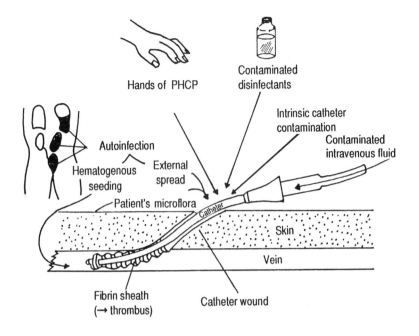

Illustration 60: Potential causes of IV-related infection.

which the PHCP will be called upon to work and the speed at which the IV must be established, aseptic technique cannot always be adhered to.

When an IV site has not been properly cleaned for the sake of expediency, the use of this site should be discontinued at the earliest possible time, and the IV should be reestablished under aseptic conditions in a new location. For the patient who has suffered wounds far from a medical facility and has little hope for immediate antibiotic therapy, septicemia would be devastating. The PHCP must always maintain the first line of defense against catheter-induced infection by practicing thorough hand washing (if possible), using gloves, and effectively disinfecting the IV insertion site.

Aseptic Techniques in IV Administration

In an emergency situation where speed is essential or in a

remote setting, strict aseptic technique during catheter insertion may be very difficult to obtain. If circumstances allow, the PHCP should make every effort to carry out aseptic techniques in order to prevent health complications in the patient that available medical resources may not be sufficient to overcome. A vital, but often overlooked, step in the establishment of an IV is the preparation of the insertion site. There is a variety of chemical disinfectants for insertion site preparation. The effectiveness of these disinfectants is in large measure a function of the technique employed by the PHCP.

Alcohol, alcohol-iodine, and iodophors (e.g., Betadine) are common disinfectants, and their usage is as follows:

1. 70-percent Isopropyl Alcohol—Scrub selected site in a circular motion, starting from the center and scrubbing to the outside for no less than 60 seconds or until the last alcohol wipe is visibly clean of signs of dirt, oil, etc. (Ill. 61).

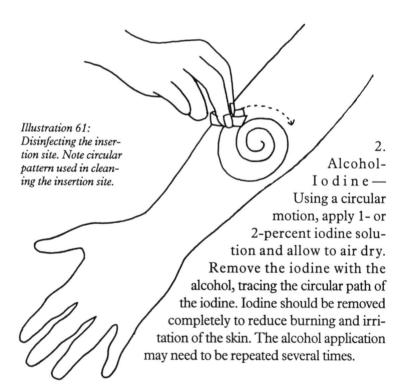

Illustration 61: Disinfecting the insertion site. Note circular pattern used in cleaning the insertion site.

2. Alcohol-Iodine— Using a circular motion, apply 1- or 2-percent iodine solution and allow to air dry. Remove the iodine with the alcohol, tracing the circular path of the iodine. Iodine should be removed completely to reduce burning and irritation of the skin. The alcohol application may need to be repeated several times.

3. Iodophors—Scrub selected site with iodophors in a circular motion, starting from the center and working to the outside. Iodophors do not need to be removed. Iodine and iodophors may cause allergic reactions. Patients should be assessed for sensitivity to these compounds prior to application.

Never go back to the center with the same swab, and never use a swab more than once. Do not touch the prepared area with your finger. If the vein must be palpated again, the area will have to be reprepared. Once the IV has been established, it is a good practice to apply an antibiotic ointment over the catheter insertion site to prevent infection. Ointments should only be used in the single-dose packets. Once the ointment has been applied to the site, a 2 x 2-inch gauze is applied and taped down.

Choosing a Vein for Catheter Insertion

Choosing a vein for intravenous infusion in the field can be made difficult by the lack of a suitable work environment, the type of injuries found, and the emotional as well as physical pressures encountered. In emergency patient care, veins in the forearm or antecubital fossea usually are explored first (Photo 36) (Ill. 62). This is because veins in these areas of the body are generally large, straight, and lay close to the surface. In circulatory collapse, the antecubital fossa site often may be the only viable vein left for catheter insertion. In those cases where both arms are traumatized beyond use, an IV can be initiated in the legs, preferably in the long saphenous veins, or in the neck using the external jugular vein (Ills. 63 and 64).

When evaluating the suitability of an IV site, the following points should be taken into consideration:

1. Choose a vein well below or above a joint of flexion. IVs in a joint can have their flow stopped with the bending of that joint. The use of an armboard can correct this problem if a vein near a joint must be used.

2. Avoid injured extremities.

3. Check to be sure the IV site is free from abrasions, lacerations, lesions, or hematomas.

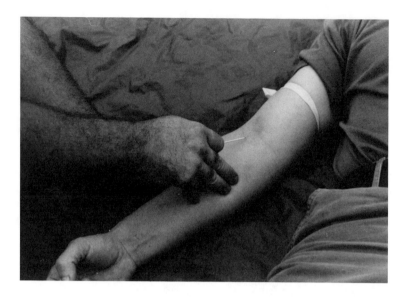

Photo 36: Note this PHCP's use of the large veins in the arm to start an IV.

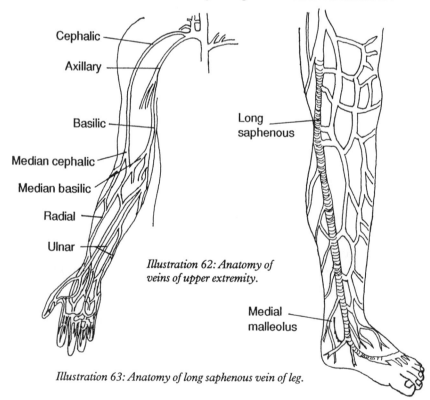

Cephalic

Axillary

Basilic

Median cephalic

Median basilic

Radial

Ulnar

Long saphenous

Illustration 62: Anatomy of veins of upper extremity.

Medial malleolus

Illustration 63: Anatomy of long saphenous vein of leg.

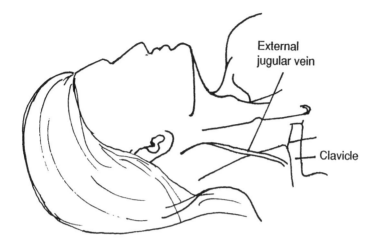

Illustration 64: Anatomy of external jugular veins.

4. Avoid veins in the lower legs due to the likelihood of complications.

5. Start as distally as possible on the extremity and work toward the body so that if further sticks are needed, the vein will not be "holed" above the final site.

Accessing the Vein

When inserting the IV catheter, proceed with the following steps:

1. Stabilize the vein by applying pressure on it with your thumb distally to the point where the needle will enter.

2. Properly align the catheter with the bevel of the needle up (Ill. 65).

3. Pierce the skin and insert the needle. There will be resistance as the needle passes through the skin, a degree of resistance when the needle contacts the vein, and a loss of resistance when the needle passes through the wall of the vein. The fact that the needle has entered the vein will be confirmed by a return of blood into the "flash chamber" attached to the end of the needle.

4. Slide the catheter into the vein. Do not advance the nee-

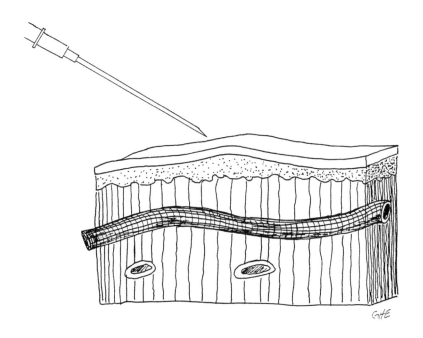

Illustration 65: Aligning the needle.

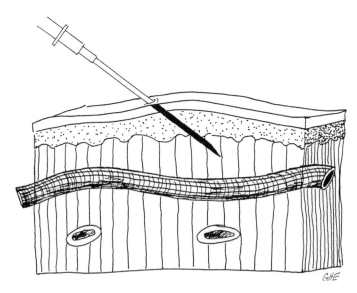

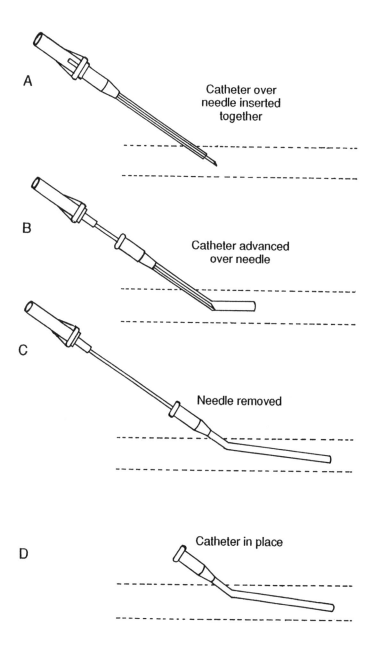

A

Catheter over
needle inserted
together

B

Catheter advanced
over needle

C

Needle removed

D

Catheter in place

Illustration 66: Catheter threaded into the vein.

dle and catheter together the entire length of the needle, and
do not push the catheter back over the needle or push the needle back into the catheter. Such an action may cut away a
piece of the catheter, resulting in an embolus.

5. Withdraw the needle (Ill. 66).

Establishing the IV ("Putting It All Together")

1. Selection and examination of the IV fluid.

If the PHCP is in contact with a physician, selection of the
IV fluid to be used is simply a function of carrying out the
physician's orders. When the PHCP is left with the responsi-
bility of choosing the IV fluid, the choice should be appropriate for the situation at hand. Once a fluid is selected, it is
removed from its protective outer packaging and checked to
see that the expiration date has not been reached. The bag is
inspected for leaks by squeezing it and checking to make sure
that the fluid is not cloudy and does not possess suspended
particles (Photo 37).

*Photo 37: Note the growth of microorganisms in this unopened but expired bag
of IV fluids.*

2. Preparation of the infusion set.

Determine whether a macrodrip or microdrip set is to be used. Open the infusion set and remove the protective covering from the port of the IV fluid bag (Photos 38 and 39). Remove the protective covering from the spiked end of the drip chamber and insert the spiked end into the port on the IV fluid bag (Photo 40). Fill the drip chamber by squeezing and releasing it until the chamber is filled halfway (Photo 41). Remove the protective cap from the needle adapter and open the flow adjustment valve in order to flush air from the tubing (Photo 42). Once there is an uninterrupted flow established, close off the tubing and recap the needle adapter.

Photo 38: Opening the infusion set. Note that the drip chamber packaged in this box is 10 drops/ml.

3. Selection of the catheter and insertion site.

Particular attention should be given to selecting the catheter and choosing an insertion site in order to achieve optimum benefit for the patient. Apply a constrictive band above the insertion site to cause venous distension. The radial

Photo 39: Removing the protective covering from the port of the IV fluid bag.

Photo 40: Inserting the spiked end of the drip chamber into the port of the IV fluid bag.

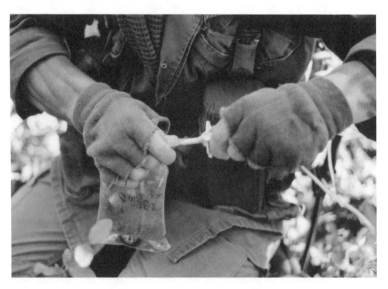

Photo 41: The PHCP is filling the drip chamber by compressing and releasing the chamber. The chamber should be filled halfway.

Photo 42: IV tubing being flushed of air. Note flow control in PHCP's right hand and the drops falling from the needle adaptor in the PHCP's left hand.

pulse should be checked to ensure that arterial blood flow to the arm has not been impeded. Once distention has occurred, take a moment to search for the best vein.

4. Disinfecting the insertion site.

Disinfecting the insertion site is critical in order to prevent septic complications. The IV site and the surrounding skin are cleaned vigorously (Photo 43).

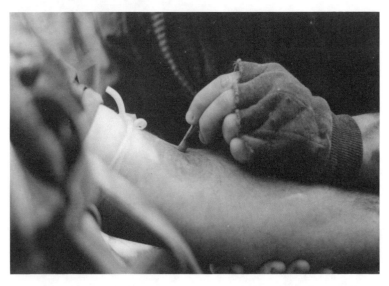

Photo 43: Disinfecting the insertion site. Note constrictive band in place to cause venous distension. Arterial blood flow should not be hindered by this band. A radial pulse should be felt at all times.

5. Catheter insertion.

When opening the catheter, be careful not to contaminate it by touching it or laying it exposed on a surface. While aligning the needle with the bevel up, apply downward pressure on the vein (Photo 44). Penetrate the skin and insert the needle until a return of blood is noted in the flash chamber (Photo 45). Once a blood return has been achieved, slide the catheter into the vein. While compressing the vein with your thumb near the tip of the catheter, withdraw the needle (Photo 46). The thumb compression reduces blood loss.

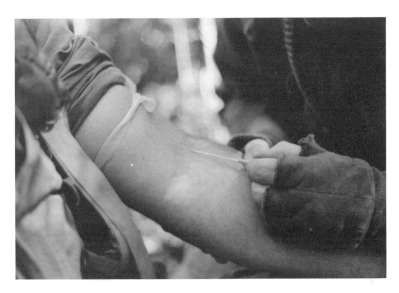

Photo 44: Aligning the needle.

Photo 45: Return of blood into the flash chamber.

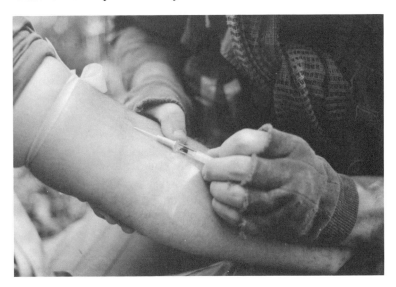

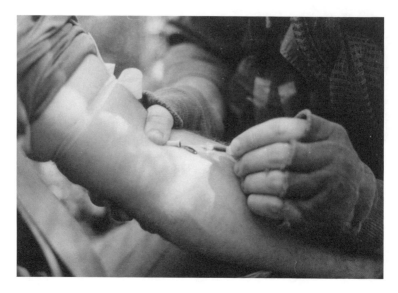

Photo 46: The catheter has been advanced into the vein and the needle is being withdrawn. Note that the PHCP is using hi: right thumb to compress the vein in order to reduce blood loss.

6. Starting the flow.

After a quick check to see that the infusion set is in order and that the tubing is still free of air bubbles, the tubing can be attached to the catheter hub, the constrictive band removed, and the flow adjustment valve opened (Photo 47).

7. Securing the IV.

There is a variety of ways to secure the catheter and IV tubing. The choice is dependent upon personal preference. After applying an antiseptic ointment to the insertion site, any one of the taping techniques shown here is satisfactory for securing the catheter and IV tubing (Photo 48) (Ills. 67, 68, and 69).

Regulation of the Flow Rate

To prevent fluid overload, the IV fluid drip rate must be adjusted to the patient's needs. The most commonly used formula for calculating the drip rate when a specific amount of

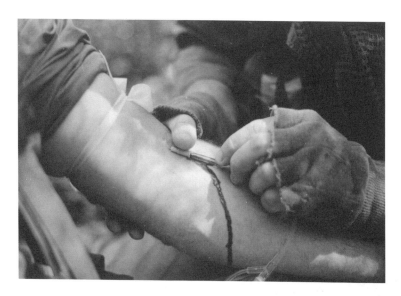

Photo 47: Needle adapter being attached to the catheter hub. The constrictive band will now be removed and the IV fluid allowed to follow to ensure it was a good "stick."

Photo 48: Securing the IV.

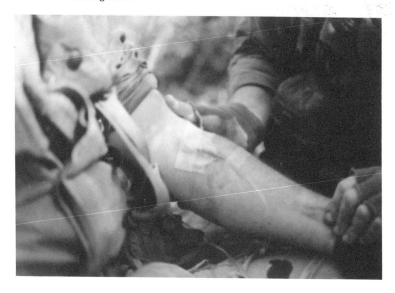

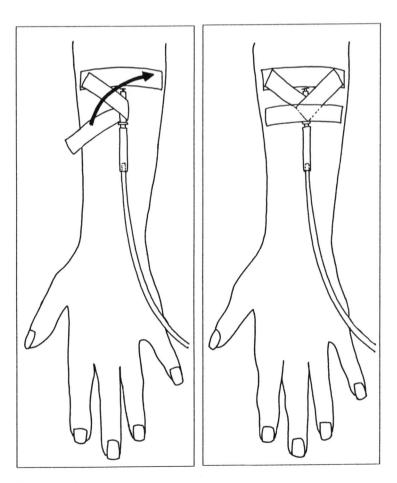

Illustration 67

fluid is to be infused in a certain amount of time requires that
the PHCP know the volume of fluid that is to be infused in
ml, the time over which the volume is to be infused, and the
rate at which fluid is delivered by the particular drip set being
used. The formula is set up as follows:

$$\frac{\text{volume to be infused x drops/ml of drip set}}{\text{time span over which the infusion is to take place in minutes}} = \frac{\text{flow rate}}{\text{in drops/min.}}$$

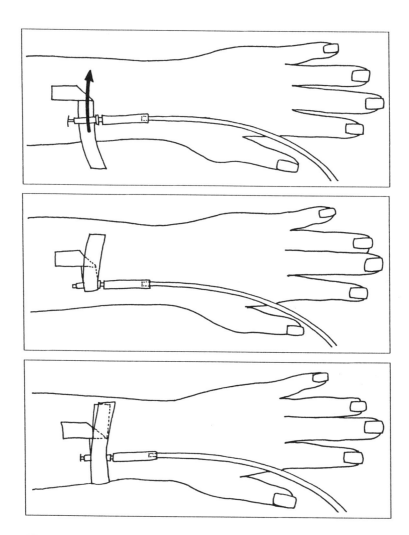

Illustration 68

The PHCP now simply counts the number of drips in the drip chamber per minute, making adjustments as needed.

Drawing a Blood Sample

Prior to beginning the flow of the IV fluids, it is useful to obtain a blood sample for emergency department use in those rare occur-

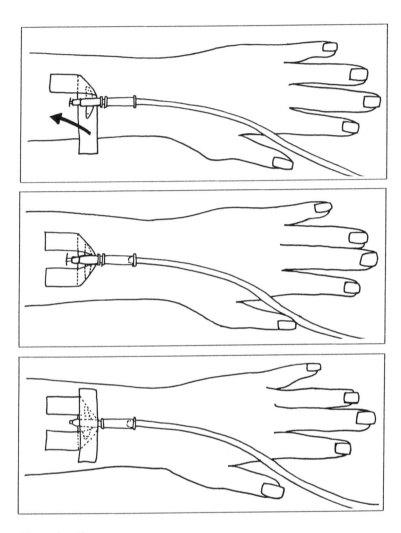

Illustration 69

rences where transport to a hospital will be short. The blood will lose its usefulness for lab studies within a short period, so chilling it with an ice pack will give the PHCP a little more time (Photo 49).

Use of the Intermittent Needle Therapy (INT)

After establishing an IV, there are situations that arise in

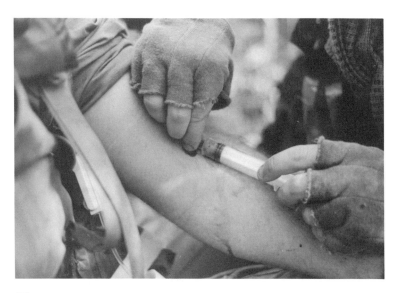

Photo 49: Blood sample being drawn through the IV catheter. The blood sample must be drawn prior to flowing the IV fluid into the vein, since the IV fluid will flush the vein of blood.

which the ability to administer IV fluids needs to be maintained, but the flow of fluids needs to be stopped temporarily. Such a situation commonly occurs when the patient must be transported over difficult terrain. The dangling tubes and IV bags become unwieldy, and, inevitably, the catheter is pulled from the vein, requiring another stick.

The INT provides a means by which to "plug" the catheter, thus saving it for later use. Reestablishment of fluid treatment becomes simply a function of reattaching the IV tubing to the INT hub via a needle. Once in place, the INT should be flushed with Heprin or Normal Saline to help reduce the chance of the catheter clogging up with blood (Photo 50). When the patient is transported over difficult terrain and an INT is not available or the PHCP wishes the IV flow to continue, placing the IV bag under the patient's shoulders will pressure-infuse the fluid. This is a makeshift approach and therefore should be monitored closely (Photo 51).

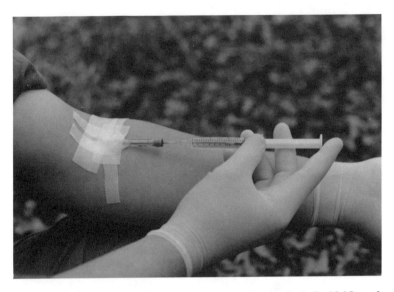

Photo 50: With the INT or "male plug" in place, it is being flushed with Normal Saline to reduce the chances that it may become clogged with blood.

Photo 51: The IV bag placed under the patient's shoulder in this litter carry is an expedient method for securing the IV apparatus while at the same time maintaining fluid flow.

The Piggyback Technique

The most common form of IV drug administration is via the piggyback technique. The piggyback technique refers to a bag of IV fluids, generally in the 50- to 250-ml capacity, in which the drug to be administered is mixed. D5W is the IV fluid of choice in a piggyback arrangement due to its compatibility with most drugs. This secondary IV is infused through the mainline IV tubing by connection to the mainline IV tubing drug port (Photo 52). The piggyback technique removes the need for another insertion site.

Photo 52: Connecting the piggybacked IV fluids to the main-line IV drug port.

Once the piggyback solution is attached to the main-line IV drug port, it is raised higher than the main IV bag, the main line IV tubing is clamped off above the drug port, and, as with the regular IV drip chamber, the piggyback drip chamber (a microdrip chamber is always used with the piggyback) is checked to ensure correct flow rate (Photo 53) (see Ill. 59).

Photo 53: Smaller piggybacked fluids in relation to the main-line fluids. Note that the piggybacked fluids are placed higher than the main IV fluids.

The External Jugular as an Insertion Site

For the severely traumatized patient, there is no quicker way to infuse large volumes of IV fluid than by the external jugular route. However, a stick in the neck carries with it hazards not encountered with other insertion sites. Anatomically, the external jugular vein lies below the ear and behind the angle of the mandible. It passes downward and obliquely backward across the surface of the sternomastoid muscle and then travels into deep fascia (see Ill. 64). Due to this vein's location in the neck, precaution must be taken not to damage vital structures that lie nearby.

When attempting to establish an IV in the external jugular, first lay the patient on his back, head down, in order to fill the vein. After the patient's head is turned toward the opposite side, the catheter is aligned with the vein, pointing in the direction of the heart. The external jugular is tourniqueted by applying one finger above the clavicle. Once the vein has distended, the venipuncture is made midway between the angle of the jaw and the mid-clavicular line (Photo 54).

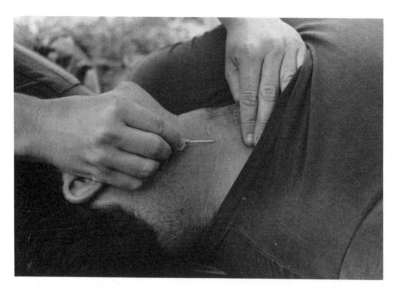

Photo 54: Aligning the needle for an external jugular stick. Note that the needle points in the direction of the heart and that the PHCP is using his left hand to "tourniquet" the vein.

Subcutaneous Infusion of Fluids

The subcutaneous channel of fluid infusion is an exceptionally old approach. A much less effective method than that of the intravenous route, it has in large measure fallen from use. It is only mentioned in this text as a stop-gap alternative for those circumstances in which a vein cannot be obtained.

In order to carry out the subcutaneous infusion of fluids, the IV fluid is injected through a needle inserted just under the skin into loose subcutaneous tissue. The fluid is then slowly absorbed by the lymphatic system. The needle is introduced below the lateral margin of the pectoralis major muscle and is pointed upward toward the armpit. The groin, thighs, and abdominal wall are alternate sites for subcutaneous infusion (Photo 55).

Around 1,000 ml of fluid can be given at one time to an adult in a slow drip that is usually absorbed in an hour or two. Absorption is more rapid in dehydrated patients than in patients suffering from shock. The peripheral circulation in

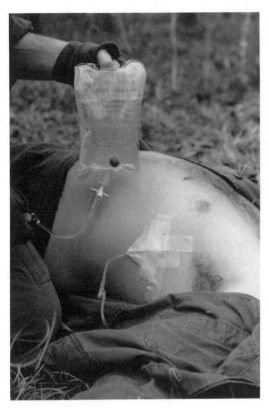

Photo 55:
Subcutaneous infusion
of fluids.

the shocky patient is often so impaired that very little, if any, fluid will enter the bloodstream through subcutaneous administration.

Subcutaneous administration of fluids should not be very painful. Following the needle stick, the PHCP can reduce pain for the patient by not inserting the nee-dle into the dense subticular tissue of the lateral chest wall, the breast, muscle, or deep fascia, and by a slow infusion in order not to cause excessive skin tension. [5]

Saphenous Vein Cutdown

When a patient is suffering from peripheral venous collapse due to hemorrhagic shock or traditional IV access routes have been rendered unusable (possibly due to burns), direct cutdown to the saphenous vein at the ankle provides a proven conduit for rapid infusion of IV fluids. [6] [7]

The procedure is carried out as follows:

1. When the saphenous vein at the ankle has been located, the incision site is cleaned with an antiseptic and anesthetized with Lidocaine (Ill. 70). A little time is taken to

allow the wheal formed by the local infusion of the Lidocaine to subside. This delay will allow the skin to return to its more natural contours. Anesthetization of the incision site may have to be omitted if time is of essence. When the incision site has been made ready, the cut is made over the vein into the fat, with care being taken not to cut the vein (Ill. 71). [8]

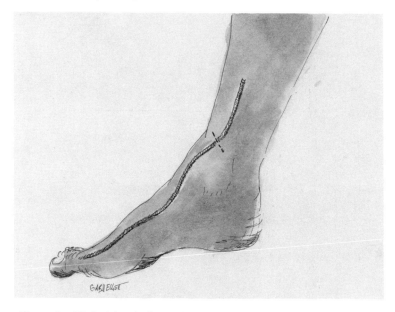

Illustration 70: Incision site for cutdown of the saphenous vein.

2. A small curved hemostat is used to spread the tissues open to expose the vein.

3. A hemostat is used to isolate and bring through the incision a 1 to 2 cm segment of the vein. [9] A sensory nerve is attached to the vein, and every effort should be made to gently separate it from the vein so that it may fall back into the incision (Ill. 72). [10]

4. A loop of 4-0 silk or other absorbable suture is passed under the vein. The loop is then cut in the middle to form two lengths of suture (Ill. 73).

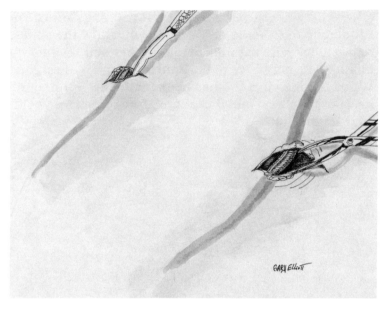

Illustration 71: The incision is made and the vein exposed.

Illustration 72: The vein is isolated and its attached nerve separated.

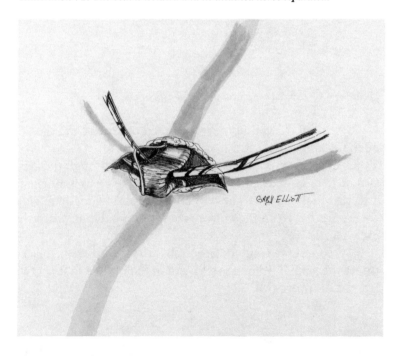

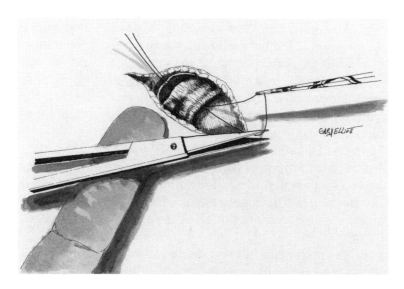

Illustration 73: A loop of suture is passed under the vein and then cut into two lengths.

Illustration 74: The distal portion of the vein is tied off and a V-shaped cut is made in the vein.

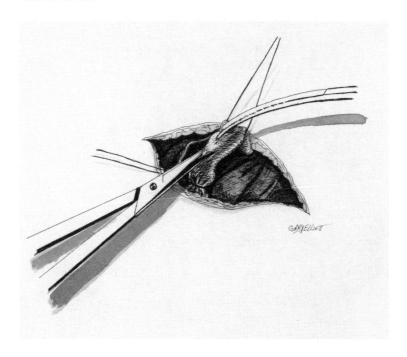

5. The vein is tied off at its most distal point. The proximal suture is not closed but used to lift the vein out of the incision.

6. With the distal portion of the vein tied off and the vein elevated with the proximal suture, a V-shaped cut is made in the anterior wall of the vein. So as not to risk dissecting the vein, some emergency service providers prefer to make a longitudinal incision with a scalpel (Ill. 74). [11]

7. The IV catheter in the range of 18 to 12 gauge is then threaded into the vein (Ill. 75). The beveled end of intravenous extension tubing (Travenol ID 3.2 mm) threaded into the vein has been suggested. [12] Extension tubing could serve as an expedient conduit when an IV catheter is not available.

8. The proximal suture is now tied down over the catheter, with care taken not to crush the catheter (Ill. 76).

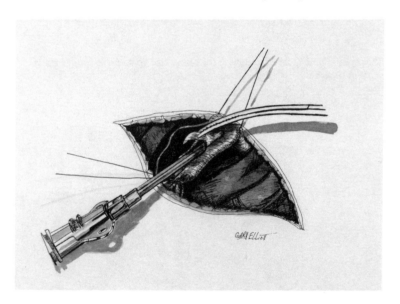

Illustration 75: The IV catheter is advanced into the vein.

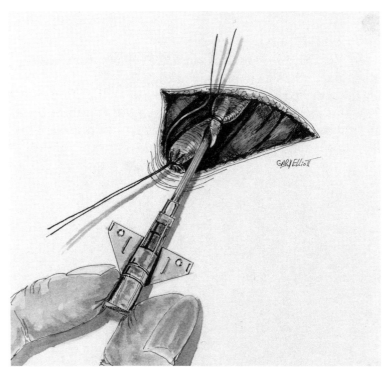

Illustration 76: The proximal suture is tied down over the catheter, securing it in the vein.

Illustration 77: The incision site is sutured closed and the hub of the catheter sutured down.

9. The incision is sutured closed. The hub of the catheter is sutured to the skin to provide stability (Ill. 77). The IV tubing is connected to the hub and the flow of IV fluid begun (Ill. 78). It is an accepted practice to wrap the IV tubing once around the big toe and then tape it down to help prevent the IV catheter and tubing from being pulled out.

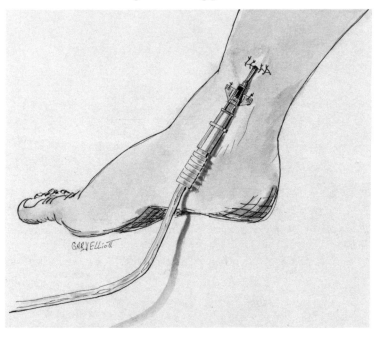

Illustration 78: IV tubing attached to the catheter hub.

Troubleshooting Intravenous Therapy Complications

Complication	Prevention	Indicators of Complications	PHCP's Corrective Intervention
Local infiltration of the I.V. site	Secure I.V. catheter firmly and prevent its manipulation	Pain and swelling at I.V. insertion site. I.V. slows or stops. No blood return when I.V. bag is dropped below the patient	Restart I.V. at another site
Infection	Adhere to sterile technique throughout I.V. therapy	Pain, redness and swelling at the I.V. insertion site. Fever.	1. Restart another I.V. at a new site 2. Consider antibiotic therapy.
Speed Shock	Closely monitor rate of medication being administered	Flushed face, headache, shock, cardiac arrest	Discontinue drug administration by stopping the flow of the piggy back
Circulatory overload	Check flow rate regularly	Dyspnea, tachypnea, tachycardia, venous distention, coughing, pulmonary edema, cyanosis, shortness of breath	1. Slow the I.V. 2. Sit the patient up
Anaphylactic shock	Determine patient's sensitivity prior to administration of medication	Itching, rash, shortness of breath, flushed face, shock	Discontinue drug administration by stopping the flow of the piggy back
Pyrogenic reaction	Inspect I.V. bag for leaks, cloudiness, expiration date	Fever, headache, chills, nausea, vomiting, shock	Restart another I.V. at a new site
Arterial puncture	Be sure of insertion site	Bright red blood spurts back through the I.V. catheter	Remove catheter and hold direct pressure until bleeding stops
Air embolism	Check I.V. tubing for holes or loose fittings	Sudden cyanosis, tachycardia, hypotension, unconsciousness	1. Stop infusion 2. Roll patient to left side, head down
Thrombophlebitis	Do not leave I.V. in for more than 72 hours	Pain, tenderness, redness at the I.V. insertion site	1. Stop the infusion, and remove the I.V. catheter 2. Cold then warm compresses

Chart 2: Troubleshooting intravenous therapy complications.

NOTES

[1] Warren H. Cole and Robert Elman, *Textbook of General Surgery* (New York, NY: Appleton-Century-Crofts, Inc., 1948), p. 171.

[2] Brent Q. Hafen and Keith J. Karren, *Prehospital Emergency Care and Crisis Intervention* (Englewood, CO: Morton Publishing Company, 1983), p. 646.

[3] Harvey D. Grant, Robert H. Murray, Jr., and J. David Bergeron, *Emergency Care* (Englewood Cliffs, NJ: Prentice-Hall, Inc., 1989), p. 603.

[4] John Emory Campbell, *Basic Trauma Life Support* (Englewood Cliffs, NJ: Prentice-Hall, Inc., 1988), p. 240.

[5] Warren H. Cole and Robert Elman, *Textbook of General Surgery* (New York, NY: Appleton-Century Crofts, Inc., 1948), pp. 162-163.

[6] Mitchell C. Posner and Ernest E. Moore, "Distal Greater Saphenous Vein Cutdown—Technique Of Choice For Rapid Volume Resuscitation," *The Journal of Emergency Medicine*, 1985, p. 395.

[7] Sam Eggertsen, "Teaching Venous Cutdown Techniques With Models," *The Journal of Family Practice*, 1983, p. 1165.

[8] Val Speechley, "Intravenous Cutdown," *Nursing Mirror*, 1984, p. 23.

[9] Mitchell C. Posner and Ernest E. Moore, "Distal Greater Saphenous Vein Cutdown—Technique Of Choice For Rapid Volume Resuscitation," *The Journal of Emergency Medicine*, 1985, p. 396.

[10] Walter J. Pories and Francis T. Thomas, *Office Surgery for Family Physicians* (Stoneham, MA: Butterworth Publishers, 1985), p. 126.

[11] Val Speechley, "Intravenous Cutdown," *Nursing Mirror*, 1984, p. 27.

[12] Mitchell C. Posner and Ernest E. Moore, "Distal Greater Saphenous Vein Cutdown—Technique Of Choice For Rapid Volume Resuscitation," *The Journal of Emergency Medicine*, 1985, p. 396.

E MERGENCY AIRWAY PROCEDURES

For those patients who cannot maintain a clear airway or are in need of emergency ventilation, endotracheal intubation is the most effective technique by which to address trauma or medically induced respiratory complications. Endotracheal intubation consists of passing a tube directly into the trachea. Once the tube is in place, it provides for isolation of the airway, thus preventing aspiration of material and fluids (i.e., blood, vomit) into the lower airway. Should suctioning of the tracheobronchial tree be needed, this is easily accomplished by introducing a suction catheter down the endotracheal tube. The endotracheal tube can also serve as a route for the administration of some drugs (e.g., epinephrine).

The endotracheal tube's most critical function is the establishment of a superior means for ventilating the respiratory-arrested or depressed patient without gastric insufflation. [1] The three general intubation techniques are the laryngoscopic orotracheal approach, the nasotracheal approach, and the digital approach. The laryngoscopic orotracheal approach is the most widely used.

LARYNGOSCOPIC OROTRACHEAL INTUBATION
The following equipment is needed to carry out laryn-

111

goscopic orotracheal intubation:

1. Laryngoscope—This is a two-part device used for exposing the glottis. The handle contains the batteries for the light source, and the blade has an integral bulb which provides illumination during the procedure. Straight blades (Miller) or curved blades (MacIntosh) are offered in a variety of sizes, and their use is dependent upon personal preference.

2. Endotracheal Tube—The endotracheal tube is a transparent tube that is open at both ends. The proximal end has a standard 15 mm connector that will fit the equipment used for positive pressure ventilation. The distal end of the tube has an inflatable cuff attached to an inflating tube that, once blown up, indicates whether the cuff is inflated. Tube sizes run from 7.0 to 8.0 ID for adult females and 8.0 to 8.5 ID for adult males. (ID indicates the size of the tube's internal diameter in millimeters.) The correct choice is the largest tube that can easily get through the vocal cords and cricoid cartilage. Too large a tube may cause damage, and too small a tube may not ensure a sufficient cuff seal. In an emergency, a good standard-size tube for an adult is 7.5 ID.

3. Stylet—The plastic-coated malleable stylet is inserted through the endotracheal tube in order to help mold the tube into a "hockey stick" shape prior to insertion into the trachea. The end of the stylet must be shorter than the endotracheal tube by at least one-half inch in order to prevent trauma to the larynx and trachea.

4. Syringe—A 10 ml syringe is necessary for cuff inflation on the endotracheal tube.

5. Magill Forceps—Magill forceps are used for the removal of foreign objects from the airway or to assist in manipulating the tip of the endotracheal tube into the glottic opening.

6. Suction—Some form of suction should be available in order to clear blood, vomitus, or other fluids obstructing the airway.

7. Lubricant—A water-soluble lubricant applied to the outside of the endotracheal tube will ease insertion.

8. Oropharyngeal Airway—An oral airway is useful in stopping the combative semiconscious patient from biting down on the endotracheal tube and closing it off.

9. Stethoscope—A stethoscope is used to determine if the endotracheal tube is in the proper location (Photo 56).

Photo 56: Endotracheal tube with its cuff inflated, syringe attached to ET tube, oropharyngeal airway, stylet, Magill forceps, curved blade, straight blade attached to handle, and stethoscope.

The following technique is used for laryngoscopic orotracheal intubation:

Double-check all equipment to ensure it is in working order. The laryngoscope light should shine and the cuff (balloon) of the endotracheal tube must hold its air. After checking the equipment, lubricate the endotracheal tube. Positioning of the patient's head is the next step. Three axes—those of the mouth, pharynx, and trachea—are aligned in order to achieve direct visualization of the larynx. To align these axes and therefore achieve the "sniffing position," the head is extended and the neck flexed. A pillow of toweling placed under the patient's occiput will provide the elevation

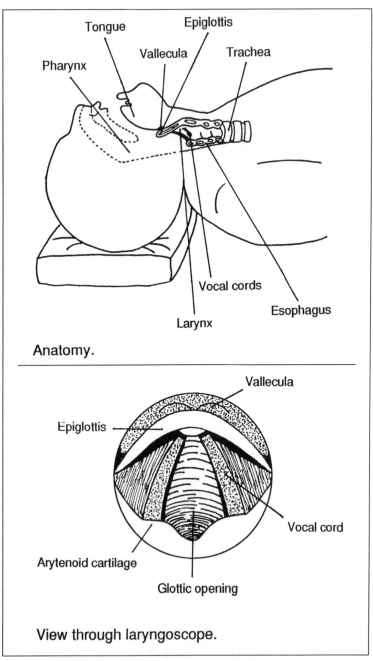

Anatomy.

View through laryngoscope.

Illustration 79: Pertinent anatomical structures for ET intubation.

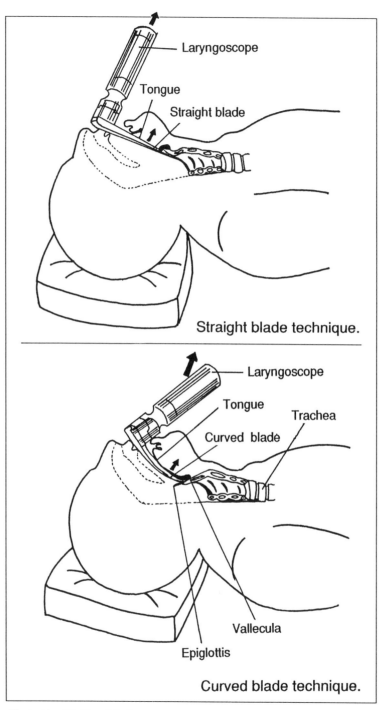

Illustration 80: Use of the laryngoscope.

needed for proper flexion of the neck (Ill. 79). Extension of the head is effected when the PHCP applies upward traction on the handle of the laryngoscope.

Once the patient has been positioned, the mouth is opened with the fingers of the right hand. The laryngoscope is held in the left hand and the blade inserted in the right side of the mouth, displacing the tongue to the left. The blade is moved carefully toward the midline and advanced to the base of the tongue. When a straight blade is used, it is advanced to just beyond and under the tip of the epiglottis. Upward traction is then applied with the handle of the laryngoscope, moving the base of the tongue and the epiglottis anteriorly to expose the glottic opening (Ill. 80) (Photo 57).

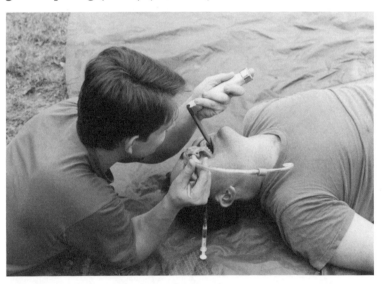

Photo 57: Positioning the patient for laryngoscopic orotracheal intubation.

The tip of the curved blade is advanced into the vallecula. Lifting the laryngoscope upward and forward at the base of the tongue and epiglottis will expose the glottic opening. Neither type of blade should be used in a prying motion, and the upper teeth should never be used as a fulcrum. Observe

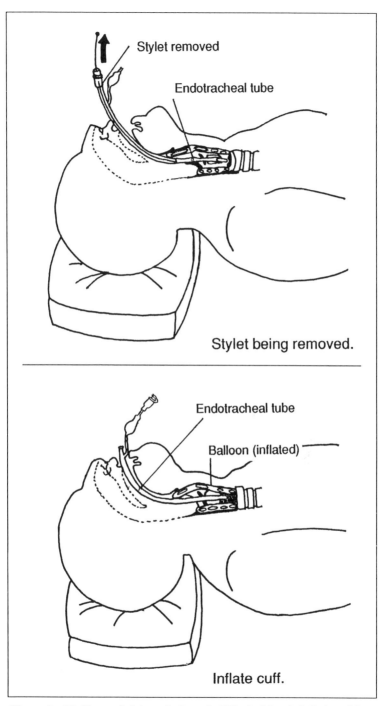

Stylet removed

Endotracheal tube

Stylet being removed.

Endotracheal tube

Balloon (inflated)

Inflate cuff.

Illustration 81: Removal of the stylet from the ET tube (above). Inflation of the ET tube (below).

the vocal cords before advancing the endotracheal tube. The tube is advanced over the right corner of the mouth and through the vocal cords until the cuff is just below the vocal cords. The stylet is removed and the cuff inflated (Ill. 81).

Proper positioning for the endotracheal tube must not be taken for granted. Its correct placement is validated by auscultation of the lungs and epigastric area. While ventilation is in progress, the lateral aspect of the chest at the midaxillary line is auscultated for breath sounds on both sides with a stethoscope (Photo 58). The epigastric area is then auscultated. If there are no breath sounds during auscultation of the lungs, or if there are gurgling sounds in the epigastric area, the endotracheal tube must be removed promptly since the esophagus has been intubated. Once the patient has been hyperventilated, the procedure can be tried again.

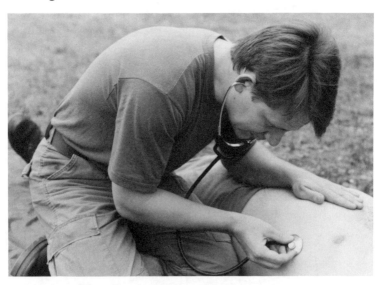

Photo 58: While ventilation is being carried out by a second PHCP, the PHCP in this photo is listening for breath sounds in the chest. Note that his hand is on the patient's chest to feel for its rise and fall, and his eyes are focused on the chest in order to confirm other indicators.

Photo 59: Patient ventilation via mouth to tube.

Photo 60: Patient ventilation via bag valve to ET tube. Note orophrangeal airway is inserted and the ET tube is positioned properly to the side of the mouth.

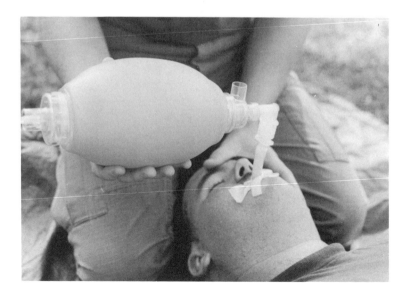

If breath sounds are heard only in the right lung, the endotracheal tube is in the trachea, but it is too far down and lodged in the right mainstem bronchus. In such a case, simply pull back on the tube a little until breath sounds are heard in both lungs. Before beginning the intubation procedure or during breaks between tries, the PHCP should remember to hyperventilate the patient. Once the patient has been intubated, he can be ventilated easily via the mouth-to-tube or bag-valve-mask-to-tube approach (Photos 59 and 60).

NASOTRACHEAL INTUBATION

Due to the difficulty associated with the nasotracheal form of intubation, it may only be justified when the patient's mouth cannot be opened because of clenched jaws, a suspected neck injury, or when lack of equipment restricts the PHCP to this approach. Since there is no visualization of the glottic opening in this form of intubation, guidance of the ET tube is dependent upon the PHCP perceiving the intensity of the patient's

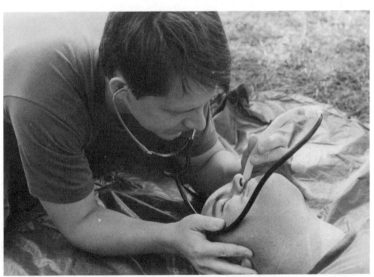

Photo 61: Nasotracheal intubation of a patient. A stethoscope has been taped to the end of the ET tube to assist in proper placement. This technique is used when a laryngoscope is not available or a neck injury is suspected.

exhalations. Bulging and anterior displacement of the laryngeal prominence generally indicates that the endotracheal tube has entered the glottic opening. Correct endotracheal tube placement is checked by holding a hand over or placing an ear over the opening of the endotracheal tube to detect airflow as well as auscultation of breath sounds (Photo 61).

DIGITAL INTUBATION

Before the advent of the laryngoscope, endotracheal intubation was performed by the digital technique. Digital endotracheal intubation in the field is useful in those patients who have suffered facial injuries that distort anatomy, have bleeding or fluid buildup that obstructs visualization of the glottic opening, or are at risk of having suffered a cervical spine injury. The technique is based upon the simple approach of feeling the epiglottis with the fingers and then slipping the endotracheal tube through the glottic opening (Ill. 82).

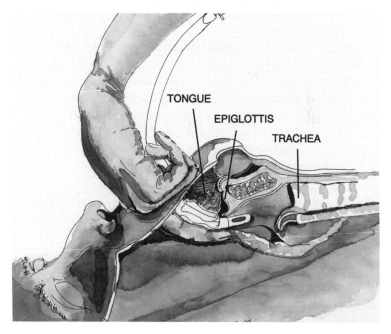

Illustration 82: Digital intubation.

The PHCP kneels at the patient's left shoulder, facing the patient. The endotracheal tube is lubricated, shaped in the form of a J, and the stylet is slid down the tube. The PHCP places the index and middle fingers of his left hand down the midline of the tongue. This movement should also be augmented with a pulling forward on the tongue and jaw in order to lift the epiglottis up within reach of the middle finger. Once the epiglottis is reached, it is pressed forward with the middle finger. With his right hand, the PHCP then inserts the endotracheal tube into the mouth. The index finger of the left hand is used to keep the endotracheal tube tip against the side of the middle finger. With the middle finger keeping the epiglottis out of the way and the index finger used to keep the endotracheal tip against the side of the middle finger, the endotracheal tube is advanced by the right hand into the glottic opening.

Confirming Proper Endotracheal Tube Placement

Endotracheal intubation in the field is a crucial emergency airway skill that can have tragic consequences if esophageal intubation goes unrecognized. In such a case, the airway is not protected and ventilation efforts are useless. To confirm proper endotracheal tube placement, attention to the following signs are used to identify endotracheal tube location. The PHCP should not depend upon only one sign but rather upon a combination of signs that will be determined by the intubation approach used.

1. The most reliable sign is visualization of the endotracheal tube passing through the glottic opening. Although the most reliable, it is not applicable in all intubation techniques and may be difficult to ascertain in the patient suffering facial trauma or in whom the head and neck are immobilized due to suspected cervical spine injury.

2. An anterior displacement of the laryngeal prominence may be seen as the endotracheal tube passes into the trachea.

3. Phonation is a sign that the endotracheal tube is misplaced into the esophagus.

4. Auscultation for breath sounds is done on the right and left apex and midaxillary areas, as well as in the sternal notch. Ventilation should result in breath sounds being heard in both lungs. The epigastrium should be silent because gurgling sounds would indicate that ventilated air is passing into the stomach.

5. Palpation/visualization of the chest wall as ventilation is carried out will result in the PHCP being able to see and feel the chest wall rise and fall if the endotracheal tube is properly placed.

6. The cynotic patient should have improved color as the result of correct endotracheal tube placement.

Securing the Endotracheal Tube

Endotracheal tubes are dislodged easily in the field. Once the endotracheal tube is in proper position and ventilation is in progress, an oropharyngeal airway is inserted to prevent the patient from biting down on the tube. The patient's face is dried off so that tape run around the neck and endotracheal tube will adhere. The endotracheal tube's final placement should be in the corner of the mouth.

CRICOTHYROIDOTOMY

There are situations that arise, particularly in the field, in which respiratory ventilation of a patient cannot be accomplished with intubation through the mouth or nose. When all other efforts fail, the insertion of an endotracheal tube through the cricothyroid membrane is an accepted approach for establishing an emergency airway. The cricothyroid membrane is an acceptable insertion site because there are no important organs or vessels between the skin and the airway that can be damaged, and it is easy to locate anatomically.

The cricothyroidotomy is begun by placing a pillow under the shoulders of the patient and hyperextending his neck. The PHCP now locates the thyroid and cricoid cartilages. The indentation felt just below the thyroid cartilage and just above the cricoid cartilage is the appropriate site for scalpel incision of the cricothyroid membrane (Ill. 83).

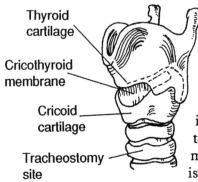

Thyroid cartilage

Cricothyroid membrane

Cricoid cartilage

Tracheostomy site

Illustration 83: Pertinent anatomical structures for a cricothyroidotomy.

The skin and cricothyroid membrane are punctured in the midline, with the incision extended about 1 cm toward each side in a transverse manner. The endotracheal tube is inserted until the cuff is no longer seen (Ills. 84 and 85). The cuff is inflated just enough to stop air from leaking around the tube when ventilation is in progress (Photo 62). If the patient is conscious, the insertion site should be anesthetized if the situation at hand will allow for this delay.

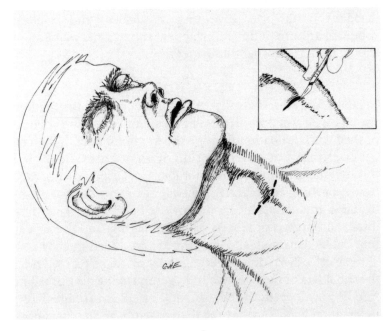

Illustration 84: Incision of the cricothyroid membrane.

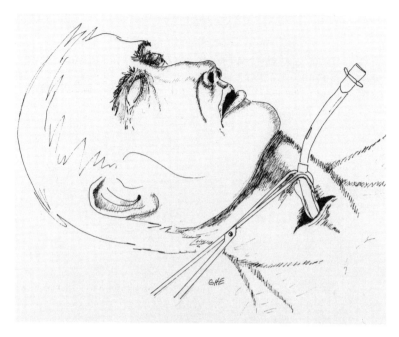

Illustration 85: Tube insertion into the "crico" opening.

Photo 62: Mouth-to-tube ventilation following a cricothyroidotomy.

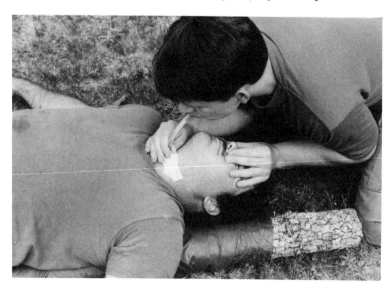

NOTES

[1] *Textbook of Advanced Cardiac Life Support* (American Heart Association, 1987), p. 30.

CHAPTER 6

ANAPHYLACTIC SHOCK

Anaphylactic shock is categorized as a "true emergency." It is a life-threatening medical emergency whose onset can be rapid. Anaphylactic shock occurs when a person is exposed to something to which he is extremely allergic. For the PHCP who must work in remote environments and who is employing advanced techniques such as drug therapy, it is essential to be able to recognize and correct the development of anaphylactic shock.

After exposure to the offending antigen, possibly an insect bite or administered medication, the patient may develop a range of signs and symptoms, including shortness of breath, hypotension, cyanosis, rashes, dizziness, nausea, hives, and unconsciousness. When death does occur, it is usually the result of upper airway obstruction or shock. Anaphylactic shock requires the injection of medication to combat the allergic reaction, establishment of an IV, and, possibly, endotracheal intubation if the airway is swelling shut.

In treating the patient suffering from anaphylaxsis, all basic life-support procedures are initiated first. Secondly, epinephrine, the drug of choice for treating anaphylaxsis, is administered, since it inhibits the release of vasoactive substances. Administration of 0.3 to 0.5 ml of epinephrine in a

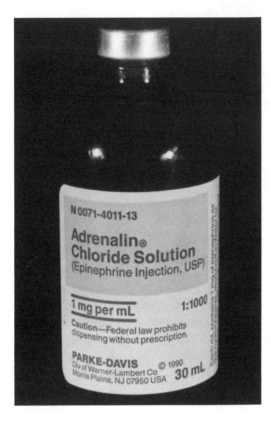

1:1,000 solution, subcutaneously or intramuscularly, should improve respiratory distress and other complications (Photo 63). [1] If shock is already present, it is more effective to administer the epinephrine intravenously in a dose of 1 to 2 ml in a 1:10,000 solution. [2]

Photo 63:
Epinephrine in a
1:1,000 solution.

    Hypotension associated with anaphylactic shock should be treated with Ringers Lactate for volume expansion. An antihistamine such as Benadryl administered intravenously will help in counteracting the peripheral effects of some of the vasoactive substances in the bloodstream. In cases such as a bee sting, local absorption of the reaction-causing antigens may be retarded with the application of a constrictive band just above the bite and injection of epinephrine into the site (Photo 64).

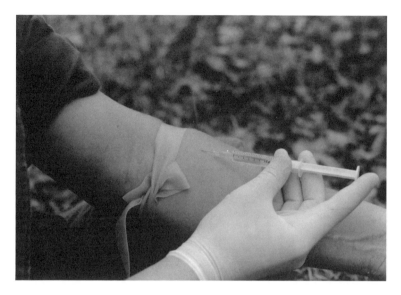

Photo 64: Use of a constrictive band just above the insect bite site with subcutaneous injection into the site with epinephrine.

NOTES

[1] Thomas Clarke Kravis and Carmen Germaine Warner, *Emergency Medicine* (Rockville, MD: Aspen Systems Corporation, 1983), p. 311.

[2] Ibid. p. 311.

P AIN CONTROL

Pain control for the traumatized patient during wound management is not only a blessing to the patient but it benefits the PHCP as well. As the PHCP attends to an injury, his commitment to the procedure may begin to wane under the cries of his patient.

During the Napoleonic period, anesthesia for the wounded soldier was woefully lacking. There is an incident recorded in which a British and French soldier were lying next to one another while undergoing operations for battle wounds. The screams of the Frenchman "seemed to annoy the Englishman more than anything else, and so much so, that as soon as his arm was amputated he struck the Frenchman a sharp blow across the breech with the wrist saying, 'Here take that, and stop your damned bellowing.'" [1]

Such patient stoicism is not often found, and old approaches to pain relief such as partial strangulation, alcohol, and limb numbing by tourniquet are now makeshift approaches for pain control. The PHCP is much better served if he is prepared to control his patient's pain by one or a combination of the following approaches.

1. Local infiltrative anesthesia
2. Administration of narcotics

131

3. Dissociative anesthesia
4. Intravenous regional anesthesia
5. Regional nerve blocks

LOCAL INFILTRATIVE ANESTHESIA

Repair and closure of most minor soft tissue wounds can be done under local infiltrative anesthesia. The "local" is simply the injection of the anesthetic into the wound site to bring about "deadening" of the nerve endings. The anesthetic is injected into the wound edges using a fine-gauge needle such as a 25 or 27 (Ill. 86). Repeated injections at various sites along the wound are often necessary. The anesthetic should be injected slowly, as fast injections can distort anatomy, inhibit blood supply, cause pain, and add tension to the tissue, which will impair wound closure. Needles should be replaced periodically throughout the procedure to assure a sharp point.

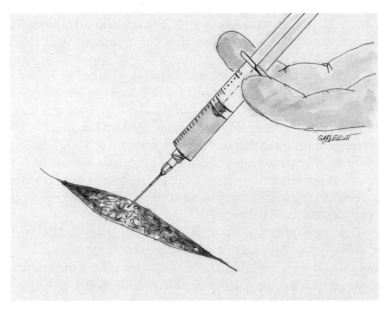

Illustration 86: Injection of an anesthetic into a wound. Several injections throughout the wound are usually needed to achieve the desired effect.

Lidocaine is a very common drug for a local, as are many of the "caine" family of drugs (Photo 65). Lidocaine is diffused rapidly into tissue. The maximum safe dosage of Lidocaine is 500 milligrams. [2] Care must be taken not to exceed this amount in patients with multiple lacerations or in those who require anesthesia in large volumes of tissue. In these cases, an alternative approach to pain control such as a regional nerve block may be more useful. Lidocaine toxicity can range from skin irritation to cardiovascular collapse. Attention must also be given to a patient's allergic sensitivity to Lidocaine and related drugs.

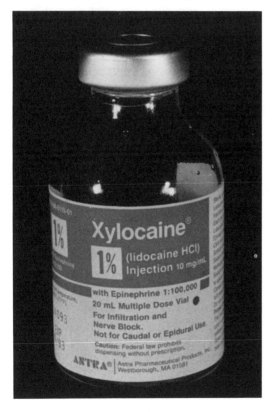

Photo 65: Xylocaine, a commonly used drug for local infiltrative anesthesia. (Photo courtesy of Mike Mitchell.)

In 1903, Heinrich F.W. Braun championed the addition of epinephrine to Lidocaine to delay Lidocaine's absorption into the vascular system, thus prolonging its anesthetic effects. [3] Due to epinephrine's vasoconstrictive properties, it became known as a "chemical tourniquet." The vasoconstrictive properties of epinephrine are also useful in decreasing bleeding into the operative site during wound closure. When Lidocaine with epinephrine is used, it should not be injected into tissue that has limited circulation such as ears, nose, or fingers, since tissue damage can result.

ADMINISTRATION OF NARCOTICS

Narcotic administration in the field has a long history of success due to its ease of administration and potent analgesic effects. Narcotics give the PHCP the ability to alleviate pain for a broader range of patient conditions and situations. Conditions such as a shoulder dislocation and situations such as expedient patient removal from the field often do not lend themselves to a "local" for pain control (Photos 66 and 67; Photo 68).

Photos 66 and 67: This patient's dislocated shoulder was manuevered back into normal position without benefit of pain relief. Note his facial expressions during and after successful completion of the procedure. Administration of a narcotic would have made this procedure easier on everyone involved. Injury resulted from a fall from a rope bridge. (Photos courtesy of D.E. Rossey.)

Photo 68: This trooper is obviously in pain as he is removed from the field. If narcotics are given to a patient, it should be remembered that large dosing will cause the patient to relax to such a degree that he may become difficult to carry. (Photo courtesy of D.E. Rossey.)

Careful attention must be given when administering narcotics since they can compromise the patient's vital signs, quickly causing the "bottom" to drop out of respirations. Administration of narcotics can be intramuscular, although the intravenous approach is preferred since it is more controllable. Morphine is usually administered by IV and titrated to the patient's response to pain control. Since individuals possess different pain thresholds, it is best to "push" only that amount of drug that stops the pain. It is not a bad idea to have the narcotic antagonist Narcan available in case of accidental overdose of the narcotic. Narcan will help the patient who has suffered a morphine overdose on his way back to more stable vital signs.

DISSOCIATIVE ANESTHESIA

Ketamine is known as a dissociative anesthetic since it induces in the patient a state of disinterest and detachment from his environment. [4] Ketamine is particularly useful for anesthetizing the severely traumatized patient because, unlike many anesthetics, it is less likely to produce hypotension. [5] Ketamine has been used with success in the following types of procedures: [6]

1. Debridement and dressing changes in burn patients
2. Superficial surgical procedures
3. Dental extractions
4. Amputations
5. Closed reductions and manipulation of fractures

When administered via the intravenous route, the initial dose of Ketamine may range from 1 milligram to 4.5 milligrams per kilogram of body weight. [7] Ketamine injected intramuscularly is generally given in a range of 6.5 to 13 milligrams per kilogram of body weight. [8] Ketamine is fast-acting, with anesthesia lasting only a short time. A dose of 2 milligrams per kilogram of body weight usually produces anesthesia within 30 seconds and lasts 5 to 10 minutes. [9] Should additional anesthesia be needed, further administration of Ketamine can be titrated to the patient's response. As with any form of anesthetic, the PHCP must be attentive to fluctuations in the patient's vital signs and the proper maintenance of an airway.

INTRAVENOUS REGIONAL ANESTHESIA

The use of intravenous regional anesthesia as advanced by Bier in 1908 is described as a relatively safe method of obtaining extremity anesthesia. [10] With a combination of bloodless exsanguination in the injured limb, inflation of a pneumatic tourniquet, and injection of a local anesthetic below the tourniquet, the anesthetic is confined to the area of injury, thus bringing about anesthesia.

Applied more often to the arm than to the leg, intravenous regional anesthesia is indicated for brief procedures (under 40 to 60 minutes in duration) ranging from manipulation of fractures to surgical procedures such as removal of foreign bodies and repair of lacerations. [11] The procedure is begun by inserting an IV catheter (plugged with a male adaptor) distally and as near to the wound site as possible. A blood pressure cuff used as a pneumatic tourniquet is now placed on the arm for operations to the forearm or hand and to the calf for operations to the foot. The blood pressure cuff is not inflated at this time.

Once the IV catheter and blood pressure cuff are in place, bloodless exsanguination is carried out by elevating the limb for several minutes. With the limb still elevated, it is wrapped tightly with an Esmarch bandage (rubber bandage) or Ace wrap, beginning distally to the wound site and ending at the blood pressure cuff (Photo 69). [12] The blood pressure cuff is quickly inflated to 50 to 150 mm Hg above the patient's systolic pressure. [13] With the blood pressure cuff left inflated and the Ace wrap removed, the limb should take on a mottled, cadaveric appearance.

Lidocaine in a 0.5-percent concentration is administered in a dosage of 3 milligrams per kilogram of body weight [14] [15] (Photo 70). The injected Lidocaine spreads through the venous system and then diffuses into the tissues. The desired

Photo 69: Bloodless exsanguination of the arm by use of limb elevation and Ace wrap.

level of analgesia will develop in 10 to 15 minutes in those areas of the limb below the blood pressure cuff. [16] Lidocaine with epinephrine added should not be used, as it may restrict proper diffusion into the tissues. The inflated blood pressure cuff should not be left in place longer than 60 minutes; tourniquet pain, however, which usually develops after 40 minutes, will probably require removal of the blood pressure cuff. [17][18] It is this tourniquet tolerance on the patient's part that has the greatest impact upon the duration of anesthesia. Occasionally, a tourniquet "wheel" of local anesthetic can be used to prolong tourniquet use. A "wheel" of subcutaneous anesthetic is inject-ed just proximal to the blood pressure cuff application site cir-cumferentially about the limb. [19]

Following removal of the blood pressure cuff due to com-pletion of the operation or the onset of tourniquet pain, sensa-tion returns and paralysis disappears in just a few minutes. The use of a double-cuffed tourniquet generally does not bring about the onset of tourniquet pain as quickly as that of

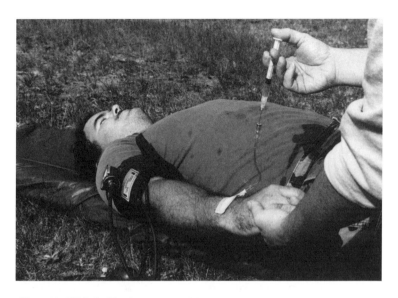

Photo 70: With the blood pressure cuff inflated to restrict blood flow, the anesthetic is being injected via IV.

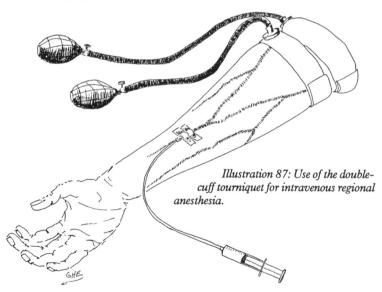

Illustration 87: Use of the double-cuff tourniquet for intravenous regional anesthesia.

the single-cuffed blood pressure cuff. In the double-cuff arrangement, the proximal cuff is inflated first, then the local anesthetic injected. Once analgesia has been obtained, the distal cuff is inflated over what is now a "deadened" area. The proximal cuff is then deflated (Ill. 87).

When the PHCP has completed the operation, he should not deflate the blood pressure cuff (tourniquet) until at least 20 to 30 minutes have passed from the time that the Lidocaine was injected. [20] Deflation of the cuff prior to this time span may result in toxic concentrations of Lidocaine being released into the bloodstream.

REGIONAL NERVE BLOCK

The regional nerve block is used when there is a need for long-lasting anesthesia over a rather large but specific area with a minimum amount of drug expenditure. Its main disadvantage to the PHCP is that it requires a certain degree of technical skill and thorough knowledge of anatomy to be employed properly.

The regional nerve block brings about analgesia by preventing nerve impulses from passing by the anesthetic that has been injected around a nerve trunk. The "deadened" nerve trunk may be some distance from the area in which the wound repair is to take place. A premedication such as morphine is sometimes given to the patient before a regional nerve block is performed. This premedication will benefit patients who interpret touch and motion as pain. For a regional nerve block to be successful, the PHCP must be precise in choosing the injection site. The anesthetizing drug must be localized in as small an area as possible and as close to the nerve as possible in order to bring about the desired effect and not cause complications.

It is a common practice to raise a wheal of injected anesthetic (e.g., Lidocaine) just under the skin surface to provide a painless path for needle insertion and manipulation prior to injection of the anesthetic at the site of the sought-after nerve trunk (Ill. 88). As the needle is advanced carefully toward the

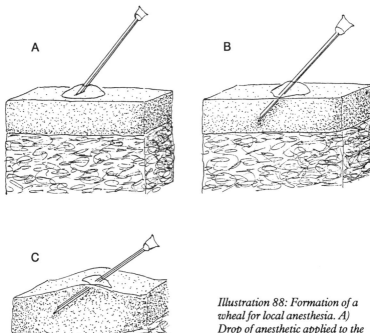

Illustration 88: Formation of a wheal for local anesthesia. A) Drop of anesthetic applied to the skin. B) Needle advanced. C) Wheal formed as the anesthetic is injected.

nerve, attention is paid to indicators such as arterial pulsations through the needle and the onset of paresthesia.

Paresthesia is the feeling of electrical shock or tingling often associated with nerve blocks. It can be painful, so the patient should be warned and advised not to move. When possible, the patient should be prepared to assist in the procedure by stating when paresthesia has begun. This will guide the PHCP in proper placement of the anesthetic. When paresthesias are elicited, less anesthetic usually is needed to bring about a successful block. However, when the needle has been properly placed anatomically and no paresthesias are elicited, several injections are made in a fanlike manner around the site to ensure anesthesia. When a block of the numerous small nerve branches that run off of a nerve trunk is needed, a circle of subcutaneous infiltration is carried out. (Ill. 89) This continuous wheal around a limb is known by names such as a garter band, wrislet, wheel, etc.

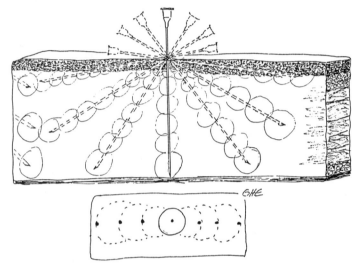

Illustration 89: Fan technique for anesthetic injection. Note that the needle is repositioned several times. Once inserted into the skin, changes in needle position are made with a slight withdrawal, then reinserted. The needle is not removed completely from the tissue when changing position. Bottom illustration shows overlapping continuous band of injected anesthetic.

The purposeful elicitation of paresthesia is controversial because of a reportedly higher risk of nerve damage as a result of the hypodermic needle piercing the nerve. [21] The needle should never be placed in a nerve, the objective being to inject the anesthetic around the nerve. [22] Paresthesia is very difficult to avoid due to the importance of placing the needle point as close as possible to the nerve. Its onset has the benefit of providing evidence of correct needle placement. To prevent injection into the nerve, however, the needle should be retracted slightly until the paresthesia ceases before injection of the anesthetic. [23]

Once the PHCP is satisfied with his needle placement for

the regional block, he should aspirate the syringe as a precaution against injection of the anesthetic into a vessel. If there is blood return into the syringe, the needle should be repositioned before the anesthetic is injected. The needle is never advanced up to its hub. Needles can break at the junction of the shaft and hub, making retrieval difficult.

Axillary Block of the Brachial Plexus [24][25][26]

(Uses: Provides anesthesia for forearm and portions of the arm.)

1. Anatomical landmarks: Axillary artery and pectoralis major muscle.

2. Patient positioning: With the patient lying on his back, his arm is abducted 90 degrees, with the forearm flexed at a right angle and lying flat on a table.

3. Procedure:

A. A constrictive band (e.g., Penrose drain) is tightened around the arm distal to the injection site. This procedure will aid in spreading the anesthetic cephalad, thus increasing the chances of a successful block.

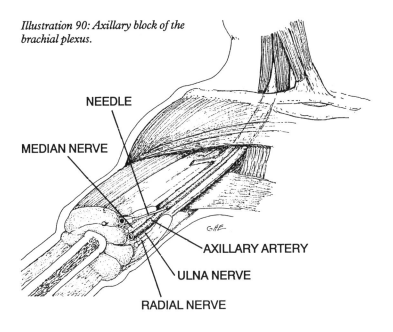

Illustration 90: Axillary block of the brachial plexus.

NEEDLE

MEDIAN NERVE

AXILLARY ARTERY

ULNA NERVE

RADIAL NERVE

B. The axillary artery is isolated and held between the index and middle fingers of one hand. A skin wheal is raised high in the axilla around the insertion point of the pectoralis major muscle on the humerus. The needle is inserted at a 45-degree angle towards the artery so as to enter the plexus. Penetration of the plexus is sensed by a sudden release and the needle will begin to pulsate with the artery. Paresthesia is another indicator of proper needle placement (Ill. 90).

C. Inject anesthetic.

D. In a few minutes, remove constrictive band.

4. Precautions: If the axillary artery is entered by the needle, withdraw the needle before injection of the anesthetic.

Block of the Thumb and Fingers [27] [28]

1. Anatomical landmarks: Metacarpal bones.

2. Patient positioning: Place the patient on his back with the top of his hand facing upward.

3. Procedure:

A. Raise an intradermal wheal on each side of the midpoint of the metacarpal bone of the digit to be anesthetized (Ill. 91).

B. Advance the needle toward the palm, perpendicular to the skin.

C. Inject the anesthetic along the area from the wheal to the web of finger on either side.

4. Precautions: The PHCP should place his finger on the patient's palm and palpate for the needle so that it does not perforate the palm skin.

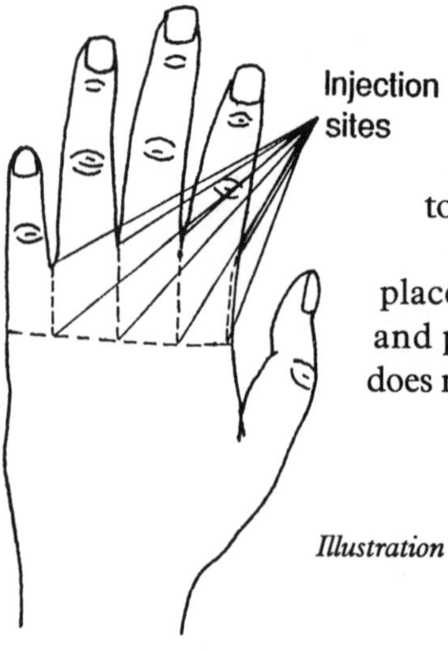

Injection sites

Illustration 91: Block of the thumb and fingers.

Block of the Great Toe [29]

1. Anatomical landmarks: Metatarsal bone of the great toe.

2. Patient positioning: Place the patient on his back with the sole of the foot in the PHCP's hand and the top of the foot facing upward.

3. Procedure:

A. Raise an intradermal wheal at the dorsomedial border of the foot alongside the metatarsal bone, web of the great toe, and at the border of the metatarsal bone of the great toe (Ill. 92).

B. Advance the needle through the wheal and inject the anesthetic into the interosseous space. Repeat the injection in a fanwise manner along the interosseous space.

C. Introduce the needle through a wheal on the web and inject anesthetic in a fanwise manner.

D. Introduce the needle through the wheal at the border of the foot and inject in a direction beneath the metatarsal and also over it toward the midline of the foot.

4. Precautions: The PHCP's hand should be on the sole of the patient's foot so as to prevent penetration of the sole by the needle.

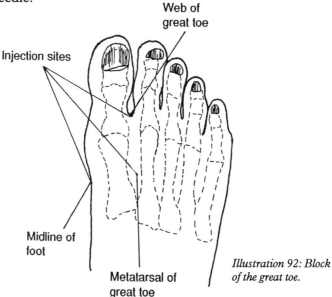

Web of great toe

Injection sites

Midline of foot

Metatarsal of great toe

Illustration 92: Block of the great toe.

Block of the Anterior Tibial Nerve [30]

(Uses: Employed in conjunction with the posterior tibial nerve block for anesthesia of the foot.)

1. Anatomical landmarks: Internal malleolus and tendon of the tibialis anticus muscle.

2. Patient positioning: The patient is placed in a supine position with the leg flexed so that the sole of the foot rests upon a solid surface.

3. Procedure:

A. Mentally draw a line across the ankle that passes through the internal malleolus (Ill. 93).

B. Raise an intradermal wheal lateral to the tendon of the tibialis anticus.

C. Advance the needle through the wheal until it encounters the tibia.

D. Withdraw the needle approximately 2 mm and inject the anesthetic.

E. Withdraw the needle slightly and then reinsert it in a lateral direction between the extensor hallucus and the extensor digitorum longus tendon until the tibia is reached.

F. Inject the anesthetic.

4. Note: A garter band of subcutaneous infiltration should be introduced around the ankle.

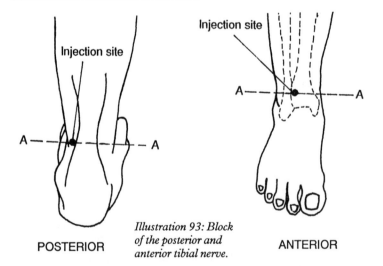

POSTERIOR

Illustration 93: Block of the posterior and anterior tibial nerve.

ANTERIOR

Block of the Posterior Tibial Nerve [31][32]

(Uses: This block is used in conjunction with an anterior tibial nerve block for anesthesia of the foot.)

1. Anatomical landmarks: The Achilles tendon and the internal malleolus of the tibia.

2. Patient positioning: The patient is placed in a prone position.

3. Procedure:

A. Locate base of the internal malleolus and mentally draw a line across the ankle that passes through its base (see Ill. 93).

B. Palpate the Achilles tendon and note its medial border.

C. Raise an intradermal wheal on the medial border of the tendon.

D. Advance the needle through the wheal perpendicularly to the skin towards the tibia.

E. Pass the needle through the deep fascia and fat until paresthesias are felt.

F. Inject the anesthetic.

Block of the External Popliteal Nerve [33]

(Uses: For operations on the lower leg and foot.)

1. Anatomical landmarks: Head of the fibula at the lateral aspect of the leg.

2. Patient positioning: The patient is laid on his uninjured side, exposing the operative site.

3. Procedure:

A. The head of the fibula is palpated, then the depression just below it is located (Ill. 94).

B. An intradermal wheal is raised over the depression of the fibula.

C. Advance the needle through the peroneus muscle toward the bone.

D. Inject the anesthetic in a fanwise manner close to the bone. If paresthesias are elicited, all of the anesthetic can be injected in this one location.

4. Note: The external popliteal nerve block is used in conjunction with the internal popliteal nerve block and garter band infiltration below the knee.

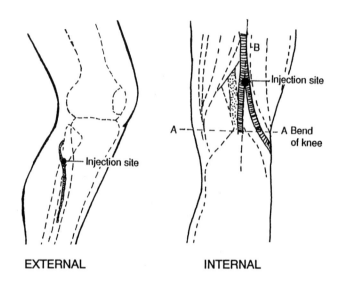

EXTERNAL   INTERNAL

Illustration 94: Block of the external and internal popliteal nerve.

Block of the Internal Popliteal Nerve [34][35]

(Uses: For operations on the calf and foot.)

1. Anatomical landmarks: The angle formed by the semimembranosus muscle and biceps tendon at the superior border of the popliteal space.

2. Patient positioning: The patient is placed in a prone position.

3. Procedure:

A. Draw a mental line transversely across the bend of the knee in the popliteal space (see Ill. 94).

B. Mark off the angle formed by the muscles at the superior border of the popliteal space.

C. Bisect this angle with a vertical line that runs through the popliteal space.

D. Raise an intradermal wheal on this line about 7 cm above the fold of the knee.

E. Pierce the deep fascia and inject anesthetic.

Block of the Femoral Cutaneous Nerve [36][37]

(Uses: For superficial procedures upon the lateral aspect of the thigh.)

1. Anatomical landmarks: The anterior superior iliac spine and the inguinal ligament.

2. Patient positioning: The patient is placed on his back.

3. Procedure:

A. Raise an intradermal wheal 1 cm caudad and medial to the anterior superior iliac spine (Ill. 95).

B. Introduce the needle vertically through the wheal and advance it until the iliac bone is encountered.

Illustration 95: Block of the femoral cutaneous nerve.

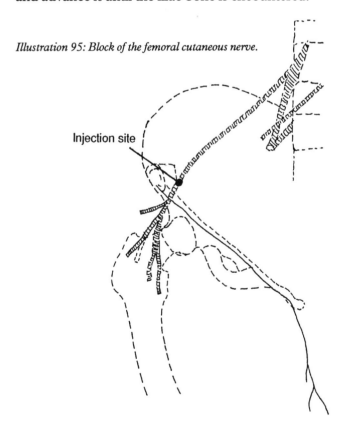

Injection site

C. Withdraw the needle slightly after having injected anesthetic at the bone and through the path to it. While withdrawing the needle, perform fanlike injections in the lateral and medial directions along the iliac spine.

Block of the Femoral Nerve [38] [39]

(Uses: For procedures on the anteromedial aspect of the thigh.)

1. Anatomical landmarks: The inguinal ligament and femoral artery.
2. Patient positioning: The patient is placed on his back.
3. Procedure:

A. Identify the inguinal ligament (Ill. 96).

B. Palpate the femoral artery with the left index finger.

C. Raise an intradermal wheal just below the inguinal ligament lateral to the femoral artery.

D. Introduce the needle through the wheal perpendicular to the skin until the iliac fascia has been pierced.

E. Inject the anesthetic.

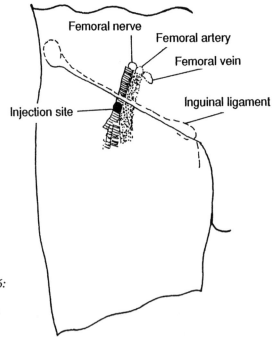

Illustration 96:
Block of the
femoral nerve.

NOTES

[1] John Keegan and Richard Holmes, *Soldiers* (New York, NY: Viking, 1986), p. 148.

[2] Thomas Clarke Kravis and Carmen Germaine Warner, *Emergency Medicine* (Rockville, MD: An Aspen Publication, 1983), p. 139.

[3] Ronald D. Miller, *Anesthesia* (New York, NY: Churchill Livingstone Inc., 1990), p. 1407.

[4] Mark W. Wolcott, *Ambulatory Surgery and the Basics of Emergency Surgical Care* (Philadelphia, PA: L.B. Lippincott Company, 1981), p. 18.

[5] James D. Hardy, *Rhoads Textbook of Surgery Principles and Practice* (Philadelphia, PA: J.B. Lippincott Company, 1977), p. 50.

[6] Parke-Davis, *Ketalar* (insert) (Morris Plains, NJ, 1990), p. 2.

[7] Ibid. p. 4.

[8] Ibid. p. 4.

[9] Ibid. p. 4.

[10] George J. Hill, *Outpatient Surgery* (Philadelphia, PA: W.B. Saunders Company, Inc., 1988), p. 28.

[11] David E. Longnecker and Frank L. Murphy, *Dripps/Echenhoff/Vandam Introduction to Anesethesia* (Philadelphia PA: W.B. Saunders Company, Inc., 1992), p. 244.

[12] Roger C. Good, *Guide to Ambulatory Surgery* (New York, NY: Grune and Stratton, Inc., 1982), p. 17.

[13] Mark W. Wolcott, *Ferguson's Surgery of the Ambulatory Patient* (Philadelphia, PA: J.B. Lippincott Company, Inc., 1974), p. 30.

[14] Ibid. p. 30.

[15] David E. Longnecker and Frank L. Murphy, *Dripps/Echenhoff/Vandam Introduction to Anesthesia* (Philadelphia, PA: W.B. Saunders Company, Inc., 1992), p. 244.

[16] George J. Hill, *Outpatient Surgery* (Philadelphia, PA: W.B. Saunders Company, Inc., 1988), p. 28.

[17] Mark W. Wolcott, *Ferguson's Surgery of the Ambulatory Patient* (Philadelphia, PA: J.B. Lippincott Company, Inc., 1974), p. 30.

[18] David E. Longnecker and Frank L. Murphy, *Dripps/ Echenhoff/Vandam Introduction to Anesthesia* (Philadelphia, PA: W.B. Saunders Company, Inc., 1992), p. 244.

[19] Steve Barnes, Personal Correspondence/October 1992.

[20] Robert D. Dripps, James E. Echenhoff, and Leroy D. Vandam, *Introduction to Anesthesia: The Principles of Safe Practice* (Philadelphia, PA: W.B. Saunders Company, Inc., 1982), p. 252.

[21] Ronald D. Miller, *Anesthesia* (New York, NY: Churchill Livingstone, Inc., 1990), p. 1413.

[22] Stuart C. Cullen and C. Philip Larson, Jr., *Essentials of Anesthetic Practice* (Chicago, IL: Medical Publishers, Inc., 1974), p. 249.

[23] Ibid., p. 249.

[24] George J. Hill, *Outpatient Surgery* (Philadelphia, PA: W.B. Saunders Company, Inc., 1988), p. 29.

[25] Robert D. Dripps, James E. Echenhoff, and Leroy D. Vandam, *Introduction to Anesthesia: The Principles of Safe Practice* (Philadelphia, PA: W.B. Saunders Company, Inc., 1982), p. 242.

[26] Stuart C. Cullen and C. Philip Larson, Jr., *Essentials of Anesthetic Practice* (Chicago, IL: Medical Publishers, Inc., 1974), p. 256.

[27] John Adriani, *Techniques and Procedures of Anesthesia* (Springfield, IL: Thomas Books, 1947), p. 299.

[28] Vincent J. Collins, *Principles of Anesthesiology* (Philadelphia, PA: Lea and Febiger, 1976), p. 982.

[29] John Adriani, *Techniques and Procedures of Anesthesia* (Springfield, IL: Thomas Books, 1947), pp. 310-311.

[30] Ibid. pp. 309-310.

[31] Ibid. pp. 308-309.

[32] Ronald D. Miller, *Anesthesia* (New York, NY: Churchill Livingstone, Inc., 1990), p. 1423.

[33] John Adriani, *Techniques and Procedures of Anesthesia* (Springfield, IL: Thomas Books, 1947), p. 306.

[34] Ibid. pp. 306-307.

[35] Vincent J. Collins, *Principles of Anesthesiology* (Philadelphia, PA: Lea and Febiger, 1976), p. 999.

[36] John Adriani, *Techniques and Procedures of Anesthesia*

(Springfield, IL: Thomas Books, 1947), pp. 302-303.

[37] Vincent J. Collins, *Principles of Anesthesiology* (Philadelphia, PA: Lea and Febiger, 1976), p. 986.

[38] John Adriani, *Techniques and Procedures of Anesthesia* (Springfield, IL: Thomas Books: 1947), pp. 301-302.

[39] Robert D. Dripps, James E. Echenhoff, and Leroy D. Vandam, *Introduction to Anesthesia: The Principles of Safe Practice* (Philadelphia, PA: W.B. Saunders Company, Inc., 1982), pp. 246-247.

AMPUTATIONS

With the introduction of gunpowder and the missiles it propels to the battlefield, the amputation of mangled limbs became a routine wartime surgical procedure. Early amputations were not known for their success. A Londoner from the 1700s is quoted as having said, "Amputation is an operation terrible to bear, horrid to see, and must leave the person on whom it has been performed in a mutilated imperfect state." [1] During this time, a surgeon's proficiency was based upon how long it took him to remove a limb. A surgeon who took as long as three to four minutes for the amputation earned himself a "shameful distinction." [2] This emphasis on time inevitably led to unnecessary trauma to the tissues, with the consequences of infection, lethal hemorrhage, or, at best, a persistently draining stump that healed poorly, if at all.

The more enlightened surgeons practiced careful handling of tissues and the precise placement of ligatures. This approach resulted in leaving healthier tissue and thus a quicker and less complicated recovery. Of course, such diligence took longer than four minutes. For military surgeons who were confronted with "dirtier" wounds than those found in civilian patients, an amputation technique that allowed the stump adequate drainage and at the same time did not require an unusually high degree of technical skill was felt to be the safest approach to take.

The open circular amputation first described by Bell in 1788 became the amputation technique of choice for the wound suffered in a combat theater (sometimes referred to as the "guillotine amputation"). [3][4][5] The use of the open circular amputation in military theater hospitals became written policy for the U.S. Army on April 26, 1943, when Major General Norman Kirk issued the directive in War Department Circular Letter 91. [6] After evaluation of the casualties from the African campaign, Kirk found that patients in whom an amputation was left open, properly drained, and healed by granulation recovered more quickly and with fewer fatalities than those who had their amputated stumps closed early with a flap of skin.

It is quite likely that the PHCP will be called upon to render aid to the soldier who has suffered a traumatic

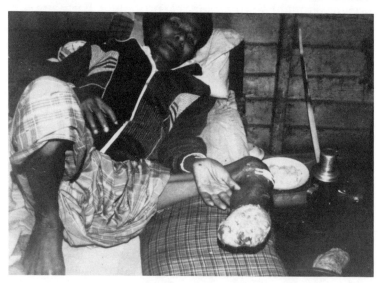

Photo 71: This 57-year-old Burmese patient lost his left foot after having stepped on a land mine. It took six days of arduous transport to reach a dispensary. The patient was a prime candidate for an open circular amputation. However, resources for such a procedure were not available. The patient is left with a gaping, inflamed wound. (Photo courtesy of Hugh Wood.)

amputation from a land mine or high-velocity rounds. Mud, grass, and fragments of the mine will be driven into what tissues are left. If the soldier does not die from blood loss, his mangled limb has now become a fertile ground for infection. An open circular amputation performed on this casualty can be a life-saving emergency procedure, given the parameters in which the PHCP must carry out medical treatment [7] (Photo 71).

INDICATIONS FOR AN AMPUTATION [8]
1. Trauma to the extremity: The patient in this case has suffered extensive trauma to an extremity. The limb has been blown, torn off, or so mangled that it has obviously become nonviable (Photo 72). In this situation, the PHCP's function is a simple revision of an amputation that has already occurred.

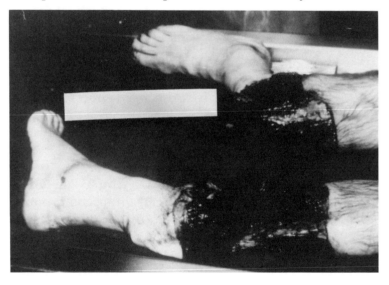

Photo 72: Amputation of both lower legs due to blunt trauma. (Photo courtesy of Dr. Gerald Gowitt.)

2. Vascular insufficiency: The patient may have been wounded in such a manner that major blood vessels have been destroyed (Ill. 97). Portions of the extremity distal to the

Illustration 97: Gangrene of foot and leg due to a damaged femoral artery (vascular insufficiency) resulted in the need for amputation of this leg.

interrupted blood flow can quickly develop nutritional deficit, leading to the development of ischemic gangrene.

3. Infection: Amputation of extremities suffering from massive gas gangrene or other types of infection can be life-saving in a field setting where antibiotics are either not available or have not been effective. Also, in an effort to remove tissue that had become necrotic due to extensive infection, debridement may have left an extremity damaged beyond hope of function.

DETERMINING THE EXTENT OF AMPUTATION

Determining the level at which an amputation should take place will not only have an immediate effect upon the ability of the stump to heal properly, it will also have a long-term effect upon the ability of the patient to be receptive to prosthetics. Traumatic wounds from things such as land mine explosions impart terrific impact forces to tissues. These impact forces can travel along muscle groups well above the sight of the traumatic amputation and result in devitalized tissues. Studies have shown that the type of footware worn by the soldier at the time of the mine explosion is a determining factor in how these impact forces are transferred to the leg. The need for an above the knee (AK = above the knee amputation/BK = below the knee amputation) surgical amputation due to mine-related injuries in Thailand was 100 percent if boots were worn, but only 29 percent if sandals or shoes were worn. [9]

These devitalized tissues, if not properly identified, may be left intact after the surgical amputation. Gas gangrene could then develop in the stump. Every effort is made to save knees and elbows and to leave as much bone and tissue length as possible. It is easier for the patient to be rehabilitated when a prosthetic is used in conjunction with a functioning joint. Also, the PHCP must keep in mind that he will be performing an open circular amputation only as a life-saving measure. It is a procedure that, in essence, is used to turn a contaminated, traumatic amputation into a clean, surgical amputation. This "clean" surgical amputation is often revised or amputated again at a slightly higher level with an amputation technique using flaps of skin to cover the stump as well as early stump closure by suture.

Presuming the patient may undergo later stump revision or "staged amputation" in a hospital, the PHCP in the field must be careful to leave as much viable tissue and bone as possible. [10] The appropriate level of amputation is the most distal level at which healthy tissue is found, given that it is fed by an intact arterial system. The incision is made through this healthy tissue proximal to the damaged tissues. It is not always easy to ascertain the true lowest level of viable tissue in a traumatic amputation. As one orthopedic team in the Mediterranean Theater reported, "'Where to amputate' sounded simple when it was followed by the statement 'At the lowest possible level.'" [11]

DETERMINING CIRCULATORY STATUS IN THE INJURED LIMB

As stated, determining whether there is proper blood flow to the wounded extremity is a fundamental question to be answered. Tests that would assist the PHCP in determining the extent of circulation and at the same time be applicable for field use are temperature of the skin, color of the skin, and condition of arteries. [12] However, these are rough measures and not sole determinants.

Temperature of the Skin

The line of temperature demarcation between the warm, well-supplied tissues and the cool, deprived areas of the extremity provide a general indication of where tissue is in the process of dying or has died due to poor blood circulation. With no instruments to measure where serious arterial deficiency begins, the PHCP will have to rely on his hand to sense the changes in temperature. Use of the hand can only be expected to give a broad indication of actual skin temperature.

To help accentuate the line of temperature demarcation, the PHCP can expose both the wounded and uninjured leg to room temperature for 15 to 20 minutes. The portions of the wounded limb that are suffering arterial flow insufficiency will become cool in comparison to the uninjured limb and "supplied" portions of the wounded limb. Next, both limbs are covered with blankets for another 15 to 20 minutes. Once the blankets are removed, the deprived portions of the limb will have failed to warm up with the rest of the extremity. As a rule, the PHCP should not perform an amputation below the line of established temperature demarcation. [13]

Color of the Skin

A patient who has suffered a traumatic wound may quite naturally have a pale appearance due to shock. However, an area deficient in arterial blood supply will usually have a cadaveric pallor. The PHCP can carry out further evaluation by pressing his finger firmly against the extremity in question. When the arterial flow to the area pressed is sufficient, the pallor produced by the pressure should be replaced with normal skin color just a few seconds after the PHCP removes his finger. Conversely, an extremity suffering from poor circulation will retain its pallor for many seconds.

The PHCP can also elevate the wounded leg and foot. If it is suffering from arterial deficiency, the limb will become very pale. When the limb is lowered, the foot may become red or purplish. It is generally advised that if this deep blush is present very far past the foot, amputation below the knee is not advisable. [14]

Condition of the Arteries

The presence of the dorsalis pedis and posterior tibial pulse in the foot are important signs of sufficient arterial flow to the distal portions of the leg. The status of collateral circulation in the injured limb is of importance, but the absence of a popliteal pulse is an indication that amputation below the knee is seldom safe. [15] For wounds to the arm, the integrity of the radial pulse in the wrist would need to be evaluated.

The results of these test are rough measures of arterial blood flow. The PHCP would do well to employ all of these tests as he tries to determine where arterial circulation has come to an end. Even in a best-case situation, this determination in the field may be difficult. The PHCP could be forced to settle for an amputation site higher than he would like. The PHCP must not overlook the fact that dislocations and fractures of limbs or pressure from bandages, splints, or swelling can impede blood flow and therefore must be investigated thoroughly.

TECHNIQUE FOR AN ABOVE THE KNEE OPEN CIRCULAR AMPUTATION [16 17 18 19 20]

1. The limb is draped so the PHCP has circumferential access to all portions of the thigh. If practical, the thigh is elevated during the amputation to save as much distal venous blood as possible.

2. A tourniquet is applied. It can be removed at that point in the procedure when major vessels have been ligated and bleeding controlled.

3. An assistant places his hands on the thigh above the intended amputation site and pulls on the skin in the direction of the hip. The PHCP holds the amputation knife firmly in his hand and starts the incision at the side of the extremity opposite to where he stands. A circumferential incision is made through the skin and the skin is allowed to retract. The position of the knife is changed as needed (Ill. 98).

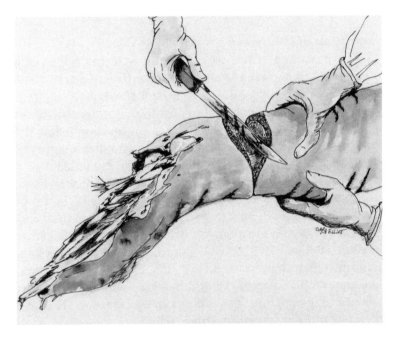

Illustration 98: A circumferential incision is being made above the knee. This incision begins an amputation that is needed due to a traumatic amputation of the lower leg.

4. The fascia is then circumferentially incised at the level to which the skin has retracted.

5. The superficial layer of muscle is cut at the end of the fascia and allowed to retract.

6. Once the superficial layer of muscle has retracted, the deep layers of muscle are circumferentially incised at the

point where the superficial muscle has retracted. Blood vessels are clamped and ligated as they are encountered. Major arterial stumps receive double ligation.

7. Upward pressure is now placed on the proximal muscle stump with gauze or amputation shield. This upward movement of the muscle stump in combination with the natural retraction that is characteristic of incised muscle tissue will help ensure that the end of the transected femur will rest several centimeters proximal to the muscle stump once the muscle is allowed to return to its natural position.

8. After the deep muscles have been retracted, the periosteum of the bone is incised and the femur sawn through flush with the retracted muscles, just slightly distal to the periosteum incision site. The femur end should remain covered with periosteum, as bone denuded of periosteum often will sequestrate if infection develops. Care must be taken not to

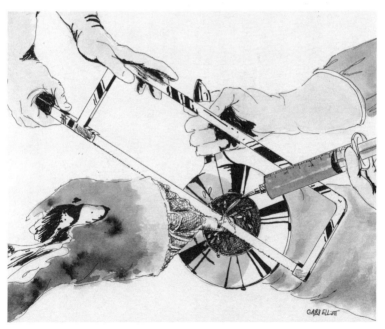

Illustration 99: Transection of the femur. Note the use of an amputation shield and irrigation during the procedure.

elevate or tear the periosteum by rough handling.

9. When the bone is being sawn through, it should be irrigated with Normal Saline solution to protect it from the heat generated by the sawing (Ill. 99). Major nerve stumps are pulled forward by forceps and cut at the uppermost level that can be reached. Occasionally they must be ligated due to bleeding. Drainage from the femur can be controlled with bone wax or gauze.

Once the amputation has been completed, the stump should be concave in appearance. The femur end should be shorter than the muscles and the muscles shorter than the skin (Ills. 100 and 101).

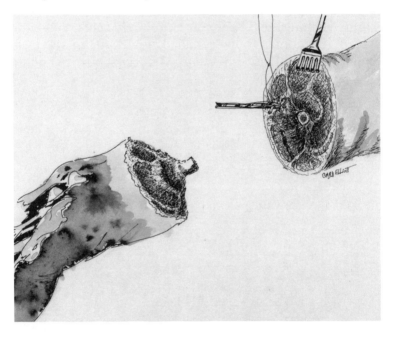

Illustration 100: Note proper concave appearance of the stump and the convex appearance of the discarded limb.

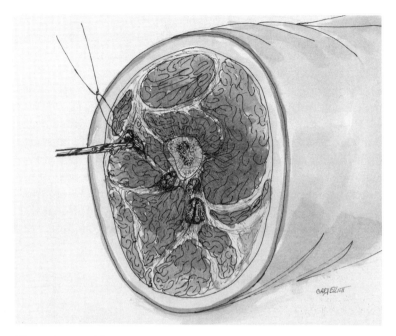

Illustration 101: Final ligation of a persistent bleeder. Note ligated major vessels close to the femur.

POST-PROCEDURE STUMP CARE

Once the amputation has been completed, the recess of the stump is packed loosely with gauze. This recess packing is applied so the gauze does not overlap the skin edges. A layer of protective gauze is now placed over the recess packing. The gauze is changed as needed, with special attention given to sterile technique during dressing changes.

Following the amputation, the prevention of skin retraction on the stump is absolutely essential. Along with the development of infection and massive hemorrhage, skin retraction is a serious complication. As the wound heals, the skin will retract and expose muscle and bone if traction to the skin is not applied. Obviously, the stump can never heal properly with muscle and bone exposed.

Traction upon the skin of the leg stump can be accomplished by placing adhesive tape on all four sides of the stump. This tape is then fashioned into strips that, in combination with a Thomas splint and additional tape or Ace bandages as deemed necessary, can be used to apply traction. The Thomas splint is only applicable for maintaining traction on the leg and is somewhat awkward to apply and easily mispositioned during patient transport.

It was found during World War II that, when possible, traction was better maintained by the use of a light plaster cast and built-in wire ladder splint. [21] The cast was formed over a stockinette that was "glued" to the skin of the stump. The ends of the stockinette were then run to the wire ladder splint, where traction could then be applied (Ills. 102 and 103). The cast was always designed to include the joint above the amputation.

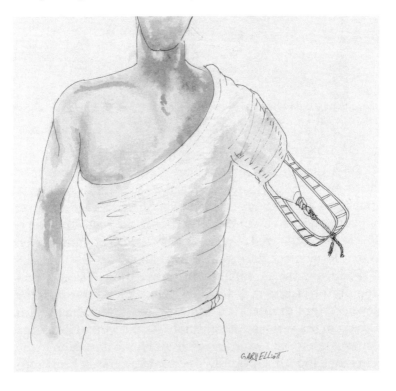

Illustration 102: Use of a light cast, stockinette, and wire ladder splint to maintain traction on an arm stump.

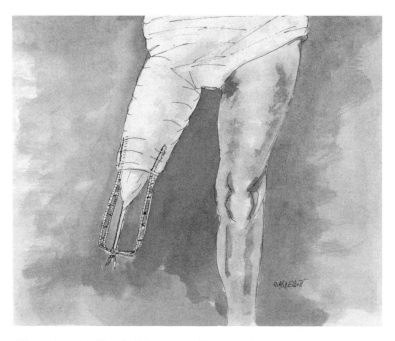

Illustration 103: Use of a light cast, stockinette, and wire ladder splint to maintain traction on a leg stump.

The PHCP's most difficult task is not so much the actual application of the traction device but the prevention of slippage. In rainy, humid environments, the traction tapes cannot be expected to hold long. Joseph Serletti's technique for the use of tincture of benzoin, Ace wraps, and stockinette is an approach that will not result in slippage as readily as tape. [22]

The tincture of benzoin is applied to the skin of the stump about 1 inch proximal to the end of the stump. It is also applied to the groin area, abdomen, umbilicus, and the lateral and posterior aspects of the spine. A 6-inch stockinette is applied over the stump up to the point of the lowest rib. The stockinette will have to be split to a degree down its sides to reach the rib. The tincture of benzoin is given a moment to adhere to the stockinette. Ace wraps are now used around the body, hip, and stump to further anchor the stockinette.

Care must always be taken with constrictive wrapping not to restrict blood flow, particularly around joints. The portion of the stockinette that falls below the stump is split along its sides up to the stump end to gain access for dressing changes. The ends of the stockinette are tied together and then tied to a length of rope. The rope is run over the bed through a pulley and weighted down with about 5 to 6 pounds to achieve traction (Ill. 104). [23] [24] [25]

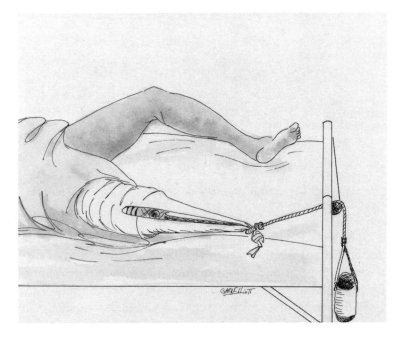

Illustration 104: Use of Ace wraps, stockinette, and weighted pully system to maintain traction on a leg stump.

An acceptable traction arrangement is one that will not slip over a course of several days of usage. It also allows easy access for dressing changes of the stump, can be reapplied easily, and can be mated with 5 to 6 pounds of weight. Even the best traction devices will need replacing periodically due to slippage. The ability of the patient to maintain personal hygiene must not be overlooked, since patients who have undergone an open circular amputation can remain in traction for several weeks.

CLOSURE OF THE STUMP FOLLOWING AN OPEN CIRCULAR AMPUTATION

Stump closure is generally carried out by one of three techniques. The stump may be allowed to simply granulate (scar) over, the skin of the stump end may be undermined enough at its edges to allow closure by suture, or the stump can undergo reamputation with an amputation technique that incorporates the use of skin flaps and early closure. It is best for the PHCP to restrict himself to the use of traction and granulation for stump closure.

When the stump is simply allowed to granulate over, continued traction is the key to success. In a "best case" scenario, continued traction will result in secondary intention skin closure over the stump (Ill. 105). Effective traction allows growing tissue to be held in place for the formation of scar tissue. Healing by granulation takes the longest of all approaches to bring about stump closure. It is not unusual for the patient to remain in traction for 14 weeks. [26]

An open circular amputation that is left to heal by granulation is often criticized for the large scar left, long healing period, muscle retraction, exposure of bone, prolonged drainage, scar adherence to bone, and reinfection. These complications usually can be avoided with proper traction and wound maintenance of the stump. Although there are shortcomings with closure of the stump by granulation, it is still the best approach for the PHCP in a forward care area to take.

The open circular amputation is often thought of as a temporary "fire break" procedure against infection that, in many cases, is expected to undergo secondary amputation to effect final repair of the stump. The PHCP would have well served his patient when, after extended transport, the wounded soldier is delivered to the hospital-based surgeon

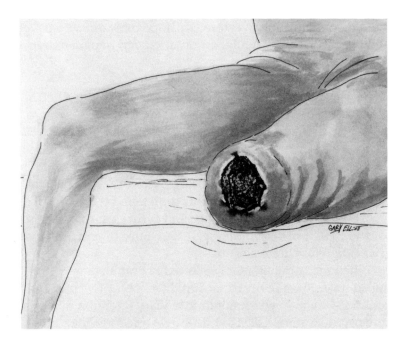

Illustration 105: Continued skin traction has resulted in partial closure of the stump by secondary intention.

with a stump as long as possible, not infected, and in advanced stages of healing. Proper traction and careful attention to maintaining a clean, well-drained stump should accomplish these goals.

A CASE STUDY

This 22-year-old laborer suffered a crushing blow to his left index finger while fitting pipe. The end of the finger was severed through the bone, leaving only a small flap of skin that connected the mangled fingertip.

The patient arrived at a makeshift clinic within 10 minutes of the injury. The finger was anesthetized with Lidocaine employed as a regional nerve block. The finger was thoroughly cleaned in Betadine. Once it was established that it was not possible to reattach the fingertip, a surgical amputation site

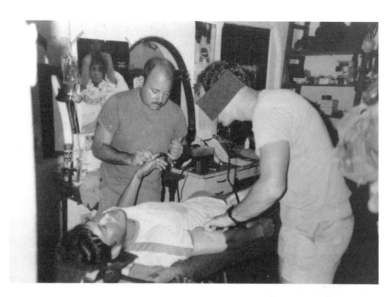

Photo 73: While the lead PHCP is determining whether his regional nerve block has been successful, his assistant is monitoring the patient's blood pressure. (Photo courtesy of Glenn Dorner.)

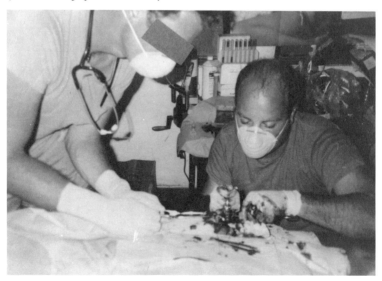

Photo 74: With the assistant using retractors to expose the viable bone, the lead PHCP uses a bone saw to remove crushed bone. (Photo courtesy of Glenn Dorner.)

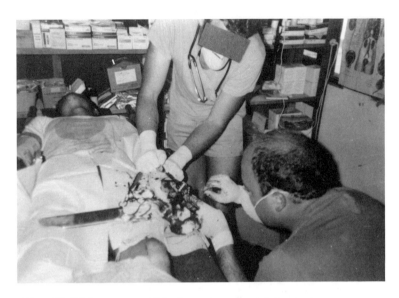

Photo 75: With retractors still in place, a bone rasp is being used to ensure no bone spurs are left. Note bone saw laying across the patient's legs. (Photo courtesy of Glenn Dorner.)

Photo 76: A skin flap has been fashioned and used to close the end of the finger. (Photo courtesy of Glenn Dorner.)

was chosen. The PHCP elected to fashion a skin flap which he used to close the finger. The patient was placed on oral antibiotics and the finger healed without complications (Photos 73 through 76).

NOTES

[1] Warren H. Cole and Robert Elman, *Textbook of General Surgery* (New York, NY: Appleton-Century-Crofts, Inc., 1948), p. 246.

[2] Ibid. p. 246.

[3] M.C. Wilber, L.V. Willett, Jr., and F. Buono, "Combat Amputees," *Clinical Orthopaedics and Related Research*, 1970, p. 10.

[4] Henry H. Kessler, "Amputation Lessons From The War," *American Journal of Surgery*, 1947, p. 309.

[5] *Emergency War Surgery* (Fullerton, CA: S.E.A. Publications, 1982), p. 240.

[6] M.C. Wilber, L.V. Willett, Jr., and F. Buono, "Combat Amputees," *Clinical Orthopaedics and Related Research*, 1970, p. 11.

[7] Kenneth L. Mattox, Ernest Eugene Moore, and David V. Feliciano, *Trauma* (San Mateo, CA: Appleton and Lange, 1988), p. 786.

[8] Oscar P. Hampton, *Surgery in World War II: Orthopedic Surgery Mediterranean, Theater of Operations* (Medical Department, United States Army, 1957), pp. 246-247.

[9] L. William Traverso, Arthur Fleming, David E. Johnson, and B. Wongrukmitr, "Combat Casualties in Northern Thailand: Emphasis on Land Mine Injuries and Levels of Amputation," *Military Medicine*, 1981, p. 683.

[10] Daniel F. Fisher, Jr., G. Patrick Clagett, Richard E. Fry, Theodore H. Humble, and William J. Fry, "One-stage versus

two-stage amputation for wet gangrene of the lower extremity: A randomized study," *Journal of Vascular Surgery*, 1988, p. 428.

[11] Oscar P. Hampton, *Surgery in World War II: Orthopedic Surgery, Mediterranean Theater of Operations* (Medical Department, United States Army, 1957), p. 249.

[12] Warren H. Cole and Robert Elman, *Textbook of General Surgery* (New York, NY: Appleton-Century-Crofts, Inc., 1948), p. 254.

[13] Ibid. p. 254.

[14] Ibid. p. 254.

[15] Ibid. p. 254.

[16] *U.S. Army Special Forces Medical Handbook* (Boulder, Colorado: Paladin Press, 1982), pp. 16.5-16.6.

[17] Oscar P. Hampton, *Surgery in World War II: Orthopedic Surgery, Mediterranean Theater of Operations* (Medical Department, United States Army, 1957), p. 251.

[18] Horst-Eberhard Grewe and Karl Kremer, *Atlas of Surgical Operation* (Philadelphia, PA: W.B. Saunders Company, 1980), pp. 426-428.

[19] J.S. Speed and Hugh Smith, *Campbell's Operative Orthopedics* (St. Louis, MO: The C.V. Mosby Company, 1939), p. 831.

[20] Warren H. Cole and Robert Elman, *Textbook of General Surgery* (New York, NY: Appleton-Century-Crofts, Inc., 1948), pp. 257-258.

[21] Oscar P. Hampton, *Surgery in World War II: Orthopedic Surgery, Mediterranean Theater of Operations* (Medical Department, United States Army, 1957), p. 254.

[22] Joseph C. Serletti, "An Effective Method of Skin Traction in A-K Guillotine Amputation," *Clinical Orthopaedics and Related Research*, 1981, pp. 213-214.

[23] Ibid. p. 214.

[24] *Emergency War Surgery* (Fullerton, CA: S.E.A. Publications, 1982), p. 242.

[25] *U.S. Army Special Forces Medical Handbook* (Boulder, Colorado: Paladin Press, 1982), p. 16.6.

[26] Joseph C. Serletti, "An Effective Method of Skin Traction in A-K Guillotine Amputation," *Clinical Orthopaedics and Related Research*, 1981, p. 212.

BURNS

The smell of seared flesh and the sight of its charred remains evoke the mixed emotions of revulsion and pity in the attending PHCP. Incendiary weapons are well known for their ability to inflict horrific burns upon combatants. The soldier who has "tripped" a canister of fougasse or been showered with molten phosphorus from a grenade represents a traumatic emergency that often affects multiple systems in the body.

With the improvement and proliferation of incendiary weapons, there is a strong probability that the PHCP will find himself caring for a severely burned patient. [1] Once confronted with this patient, the PHCP must be able to render emergency care quickly, determine the severity of the burn, and initiate a course of treatment.

ANATOMY OF THE SKIN

The skin is considered the largest organ of the body. It is described as having two layers. The outer layer, which serves as a barrier between the environment and the body, is called the epidermis. The dermis lies below the epidermis. The dermis contains the sweat glands, hair follicles, oil glands, and sensory nerves. Of particular importance to the recovering burn patient is how the dermis contains those cells responsible for the creation of new skin.

PATHOLOGY OF THE BURN
The skin's myriad of vital functions (e.g., temperature regulation, barrier to bacteria, sensory input, etc.) are easily disrupted by burns. Even seemingly minor localized burns have the potential to cause dysfunction in critical body processes. Depending upon the severity of the burn, body structures such as blood vessels undergo dramatic changes. Cell death and damage cause increased capillary permeability and a loss of vascular integrity. The escape of nonformed blood elements (plasma) into the tissues soon brings about the characteristic edema and blistering found in burns. The extravasation of bodily fluids through the burn wound in combination with shifts in peripheral vascular resistance can lead to burn shock. The patient's condition can be further antagonized by a decrease in cardiac output. Reduced circulation to the damaged tissues due to a loss of "pumping capacity" and physical destruction of blood vessels causes expansion of dead and dying tissue.

With consistency and chemical changes in the blood, loss of fluid, and shifts in regulatory mechanisms, the liver may begin to swell and urinary output from the kidneys drops. Urinary output generated may find its path obstructed if the urethra has swollen shut due to a burn to the penis. The stomach may distend, and sheared lungs may begin to fill with fluid. Finally, what is often the death-dealing blow, bacteria find an excellent growth medium in the skin that has undergone coagulation necrosis. The resulting infection has an unnatural advantage since the vessels that would normally carry the infection-fighting white cells have been charred beyond use (Ills. 106 and 107).

ASSESSING THE EXTENT OF THE BURN
The "Rule of Nines" has long been recognized as an acceptable tool by which to assess the area of burn expressed

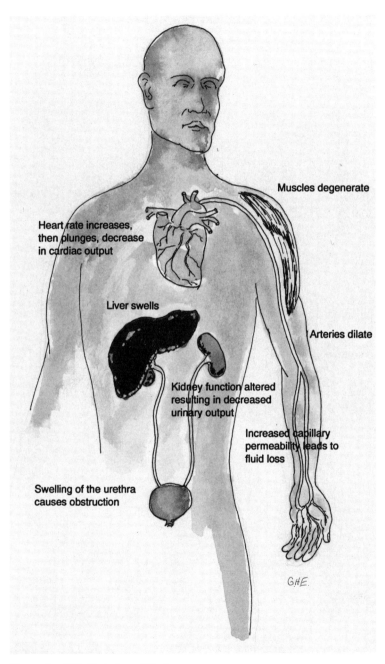

Muscles degenerate

Heart rate increases, then plunges, decrease in cardiac output

Liver swells

Arteries dilate

Kidney function altered resulting in decreased urinary output

Increased capillary permeability leads to fluid loss

Swelling of the urethra causes obstruction

G.H.E.

Illustration 106: Pathology of the burn.

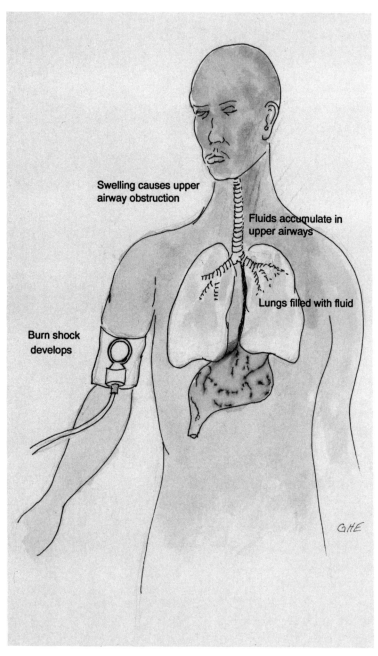

Illustration 107: Pathology of the burn.

as a percent of total body surface. The body is divided into anatomical parts and assigned certain percentages (Ill. 108). Once the burned areas' corresponding percentages have been added, the PHCP will have an estimate of the extent of body surface involved in the burn.

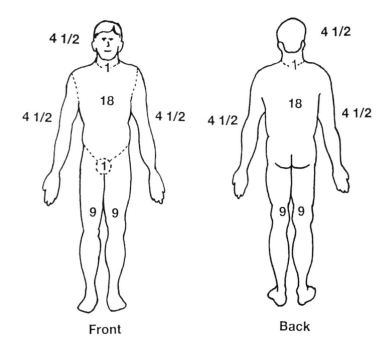

Front   Back

Illustration 108: Percentages are assigned to anatomical parts, giving an estimate of the extent of body surface involved in the burn.

Determining the Depth of the Burn

Burns have long been characterized as first, second, or third degree, based on the depth of tissue damage and tissue response to the burn (Ill. 109). First-degree burns are considered a superficial injury because only the epidermis is affected. Burns of this degree will cause reddening of the skin, and in the worst cases, some swelling may develop. The burn will be painful, but with minor care it will heal on its own without scarring. Since the epidermis is the only layer of skin involved in a first-degree burn, this type of burn is also known as a superficial partial-thickness burn or partial-thickness burn.

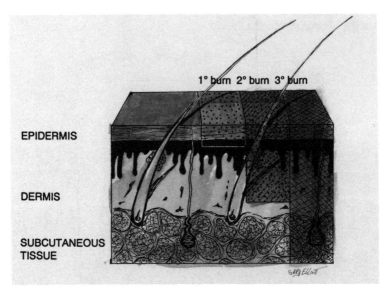

1° burn 2° burn 3° burn

EPIDERMIS

DERMIS

SUBCUTANEOUS
TISSUE

Illustration 109: Depth of the burn injury as characterized by degree.

In a second-degree burn, the epidermis has been burned through and the dermal layer has suffered injury. The burn does not pass through the dermal or second layer of skin. The patient will exhibit severe pain, and the skin will be blistered, reddened, and mottled in appearance. A large amount of swelling is to be expected. As with first-degree burns, second-degree burns will heal on their own with appropriate care, leaving little scarring. Since both the epidermis and dermis are injured in a second-degree burn, it is known as a deep partial-thickness or partial-thickness burn.

Third-degree burns damage all layers of the skin and in severe cases can injure underlying structures such as muscle and bone. Burns of this type leave charred, blackened, and/or dry, pearly white areas (photos 77 and 78). The patient may

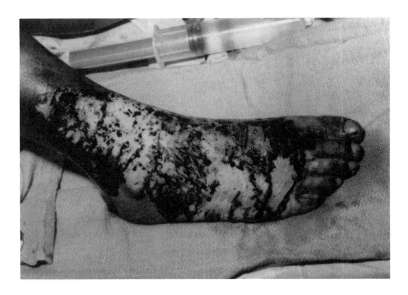

Photos 77 and 78: Third-degree burns to the foot and arm. Note the blackened and pearly white areas.

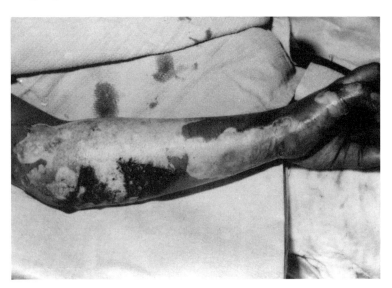

suffer severe pain. However, this pain is probably the result of nearby second-degree burns, as the nerve endings are often destroyed in third-degree burns. Third-degree burns heal poorly since the regenerative powers of the tissues have been lost. If left to its own resources, the burn usually will scar over from the edges where viable tissue still exists. Skin grafting is required to bring about proper healing of the burn. Third-degree burns are also defined as full-thickness burns, as they extend throughout all dermal layers and possibly to the sub-cutaneous layers, muscle, and bone.

Some emergency health care providers have moved away from the use of first through third degree as measures of burn depth, replacing these measures with categorizations of either superficial or deep burn. [2] Should the PHCP hear of a burn referred to as superficial, he can expect to find a burn that is reddened, swollen, and tender. A deep burn is one that is sur-rounded by reddened skin and blistered/swollen in the center. In the most serious cases of a deep burn, the affected skin will be charred and/or pearly white (Chart 3).

	First Degree	Second Degree	Third Degree
Skin Color	Red or discolored	Red or mottled	Pearly white and/or charred; translucent; parchment-like
Skin Surface	Mild swelling; dry with no blisters	Blisters with weeping; greater degree of swelling	Charred epidermis, dermis, fat and muscle; dry with thrombosed blood vessels; skin coagulation
Pain Response	Painful	Painful	No pain due to destroyed nerve endings
Causes of Burn	Sunburn; light contact with hot objects, water or steam	Deep sunburn; contact with hot objects and liquids; flash burns from petroleum products	Prolonged exposure to flame; hot objects or liquids; electricity

Chart 3: Characteristics of burn wounds.

Determining Burn Severity

Burn severity is categorized as major, moderate, or minor. Classification of burn severity serves to establish the order of care, type of care, and how and when to transport the patient. In cases of quick transport, it gives receiving emergency department personnel information upon which to base a response.

Assigning a burn patient to one of the severity categories is dependent upon evaluation of the following determining factors:

1. Degree and extent of the burn
2. Body regions burned
3. Source of the burn
4. Other injuries the patient has suffered

Degree and extent: Using the criteria of first-, second-, and third-degree burns along with the Rule of Nines, a vital measurement of injury severity is determined.

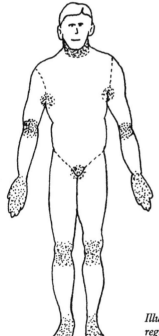

Body regions burned: Burns to the face can result in the loss of the airway and damage to the eyes. Burns to the hands, feet, and joints are of concern due to scarring, loss of movement, and, most critically, the infliction of circumferential burns with a developing constricting eschar. Burns to the buttocks, groin, and medial thigh are more susceptible to infection (Ill. 110).

Source of the burn: A "minor" chemical burn may be potentially more life-endangering than a comparable thermal

Illustration 110: Shaded areas represent body regions that, once burned, can easily lead to complications.

burn. Chemical residue may burn the skin for some time and can be absorbed into the body to damage internal organs, depending on the type of chemical.

Other patient injuries: For the patient who has suffered from an explosion, the possibility of internal bleeding must not be overlooked while treating the burn. Underlying injures must always be sought out.

Once the determining factors have been evaluated, the burn can be categorized as follows, using American Burn Association parameters. [3] It should be remembered that it may take a little time for the full extent of the burn injury to manifest itself. What is taken for second-degree burn at the scene may develop into a third-degree burn at a later date.

Major Burns:
1. Second-degree burns involving >25 percent of total body surface
2. Third-degree burns involving >10 percent of total body surface
3. Burns complicated by respiratory tract injury, fractures, or those involving critical areas such as face, hands, feet, and perineum
4. High-voltage electrical burns
5. Lesser burns in patients with significant preexisting disease

Moderate Burns:
1. Second-degree burns involving 15 to 25 percent of total body surface
2. Third-degree burns involving 2 to 10 percent of total body surface
3. Areas above not involving face, hands, feet, perineum

Minor Burns:
1. Second-degree burns <15 percent of total body surface
2. Third-degree burns <2 percent of total body surface

EMERGENCY CARE FOR THE BURNED PATIENT
The PHCP's initial three goals in rendering care to the burned patient are to remove the victim from the source of the burn, limit burn wound progression, and maintain air-

way patency. When removing the patient from the burn source (be it thermal, chemical, or electrical), the PHCP must be attentive to his own safety as well as his patient's in order to remain a useful component of the emergency medical system.

Limiting Burn Wound Progression

After the patient has been removed from the scene of injury, the progression of the burn wound is inhibited by cooling the burned skin. Burns not cooled can continue to radiate heat to surrounding tissues extending from the wound. Cool water should be applied to the wound for one to two minutes. Prolonged cooling of the burn may cause hypothermia and shock. Ice is never used since it constricts vessels, causing further damage due to inhibiting blood flow to the burn. Butter, oils, etc., should also not be applied to the burn.

Chemical burns receive extensive irrigation with water to dilute and wash away the chemical. Particles of the chemical that adhere to the skin are wiped away. Contact lenses are removed from the eyes for effective irrigation.

Once the burn has been cooled, clothing and jewelry are removed. Clothing that adheres to the burn is cut around and left in place. While the burn site is exposed, a quick patient assessment is made to determine the type of burn, its severity, and whether there is other trauma to the patient. Although the burn can look devastating, other trauma or respiratory complications are more likely to cause immediate death.

After cooling and assessment, the burns are covered with dry bandages and the patient covered with sheets or blankets to keep him warm. If at all possible, sterile material should be placed against the burn. Even in a warm environment, damaged skin having lost its temperature-regulation capacity should be covered. Burn patients should never be transported in wet bandages. An occasional moist compress for small areas is acceptable for easing the patient's pain. If at hand, oxygen and IV therapy are begun.

Burns to the Respiratory System

Inhalation injuries as associated with burns result from the inhalation of superheated gases or steam. A burn to the respiratory system is most often caused by prolonged exposure to the hazardous environment. Patient entrapment is the primary cause for this prolonged exposure. Death can be rapid as the upper airway swells shut and/or the lungs fill with fluid.

Signs and symptoms of respiratory system burns are:

1. Severe head and neck burns, charred flesh, burned nasal hairs, swollen lips, etc.

2. Hoarseness and coughing

3. Soot in and around the mouth and nose

4. Rapid respirations

5. Cyanosis

6. Fluid in the lungs

7. Stridor (high-pitched breathing)

Emergency intervention for the respiratory-distressed patient focuses on maintaining a viable airway. Endotracheal intubation or a cricothyroidotomy are the best options for maintaining an open airway when it is beginning to swell shut (Ill. 111). There are some who feel that nasotracheal intubation is the intubation method of choice for the burned patient. When the PHCP is attempting to intubate his patient, he may run into difficulty; burn irritation to the airway may cause lethal laryngo spasms when the endotracheal tube touches the laryngeal area.

Illustration 111: Heat inhalation can result in airway obstruction by swelling of the hypopharynx. Left illustration depicts normal anatomy. Right illustration shows swelling of tissues proximal to the vocal cords.

Fluid buildup in the lungs can quickly endanger the patient's life. The PHCP should elevate the patient's torso to pool the fluid in the lower portions of the lungs. Suctioning via the endotracheal tube often helps remove some of the fluid buildup.

Oxygen therapy is of vital importance in any trauma case. Severe burns can destroy the red blood cells' ability to transport oxygen. Some of the inhaled smoke may have contained carbon monoxide (Photo 79). Unfortunately for the PHCP's patient, it is highly unlikely that he has "humped" an E-size oxygen cylinder in his rucksack. When high-flow oxygen is not available for administration, the PHCP must ensure that the patient is completely removed from the smoke-filled environment to avoid any further damage.

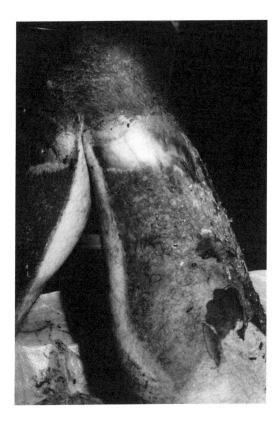

Photo 79: Cause of death for this man was smoke inhalation. Note the heavy accumulation of soot on the leg and the clear line of demarcation that gives some idea of the extent of the smoke-filled environment. (Photo courtesy of Georgia Bureau of Investigation/Photo Lab.)

EMERGENCY TREATMENT
FOR THE BURN PATIENT

Management of the burn site in the field is generally restricted to the emergency "care" of cooling and dressing the burn along with airway maintenance. Should the situation at hand rule out immediate patient transport, the PHCP must be ready to provide emergency "treatment" in the following areas:

1. Fluid therapy for the burn patient
2. Nasogastric tube insertion
3. Antibiotic therapy for burns
4. Escharotomy
5. Cleaning and debridement of the burn wound

Fluid Therapy for the Burn Patient

To prevent the burn patient from succumbing to hypovolemic shock, an intravenous line is established and Ringer's Lactate administered as the patient's condition dictates. Burns to the arms can render common IV access sites such as the antecubital fossa unusable. A cut down to the greater saphenous vein in the ankle often is the best IV site available, as it usually has been protected from flames by the soldier's leather boots.

Even if transport time to a hospital is short (half an hour or less), it is still a good practice to establish an IV. Burn shock does take some time to develop, but an IV in place at minimal flow is one less procedure to be initiated should the patient's blood pressure drop. When the patient must face extended transport times, proper fluid therapy is of great importance to prevent or correct hypovolemic shock.

There are several accepted formulas for IV fluid administration to the burned patient. The Ringer's Lactate formula provides a guideline by which to administer IV fluids during the first 24 hours after the burn. [4] Ringer's Lactate formula:

A. Percent body surface area burn x kg body weight x 4 ml = cc of Ringer's Lactate to be administered for the first 24 hours

B. One-half of the total is given in the first 8 hours following the burn

C. One-quarter of the total is given in the following two 8-hour periods

For example, a 70 kg man who has suffered burns to 60 percent of his body would receive 16,800 cc (almost 17 liters) of fluid over the upcoming 24-hour period.

To determine whether or not the fluid therapy is adequate, the PHCP needs to monitor urine output as well as vital signs. Catherization of the urethra and collection of the urine are essential. When there have been burns to the groin, the urethra should always be catherized with a Foley catheter. Groin burns can cause the urethra to swell closed, thus preventing urine from being expelled from the body. Once the catheter is in place, the patient should expel 25 to 50 ml of urine per hour if the fluid therapy is adequate. [5] The patient should also be exhibiting normal vital signs. Acute renal failure in burn patients is generally the result of hypovolemia.

After the first 24 hours of fluid administration, the flow should be adjusted to maintain proper urine output and vital signs while at the same time not causing fluid overload. After 48 hours, the swelling and growing edema stage of the burn should begin to subside. This will allow fluid administration to be reduced. If after IV therapy has been initiated the patient's signs of shock are still present, the PHCP should reevaluate his patient for other forms of trauma he has overlooked.

Oral intake of electrolyte solutions can be of help to patients with minor burns. However, the severely burned patient may suffer paralytic ileus and vomiting. Oral administration of electrolyte solutions to these patients is generally not advisable. In the absence of IV solutions, oral intake of electrolyte solutions may be life-saving.

Nasogastric Tube Insertion

In severe burn cases, gastric distention and vomiting are often encountered. The PHCP must be cautious about giving his patient fluids orally. It is a good practice to place a nasogastric tube down the patient's esophagus. This tube can help relieve the discomfort of a distending belly. Some feel that administration of antacids will help prevent the development of stomach ulcers. [6]

Antibiotic Therapy for Burns

Burn patients are very susceptible to infection. The burn site, due to its poor circulation and abundant dead tissue, easily supports bacteria growth. Infection that is left unchecked can cause additional tissue destruction or lead to the death of the patient.

Vancomycin or penicillin, administered via IV infusion, are commonly used for protection against and combating of staphylococcus aureus as well as other bacteria found in burn wound infections. Topical application of infection-fighting creams such as Silvadene Cream, Furacin Cream, and Sulfamylon Cream are effective and easily applied. The use of topical creams that possess bactericidal properties is particularly important in deep burn cases where systemic antibiotics may not be able to reach the sight of infection in sufficient levels due to the avascular nature of the wound. The antibacterial properties of these creams have been reported to allow healing of partial-thickness burns by preventing conversion of the partial-thickness burn to full thickness due to sepsis. [7]

Topical creams are applied to burns with a gloved hand, spatula, or tongue depressor while paying strict attention to sterile technique. The creams do not have to be covered with a dressing. The burn should remain covered with cream until healing is well advanced. Since the cream should remain intact, dressing the burn while still in a forward area is a good idea. This dressing will prevent the cream from being wiped off due to patient movement and provide a barrier to a less than sterile environment. The topical creams are applied once or twice daily to a thickness of about 1/16 inch. [8] The cream is, of course, reapplied after scheduled cleaning of the burn.

Escharotomy

In deep severe burns, skin protein may become denatured and hard, leaving a firm, leatherlike covering known as an eschar. An eschar presents a hazard to the patient when it encircles an extremity or the chest wall. When edema develops under the constrictive band of eschar, blood circulation to the distal portions of the limb may be restricted to the point of causing death to otherwise healthy tissue. Developing edema with a circumferential eschar to the chest is capable of inhibiting respiratory efforts. In those cases where a limb is suffering from insufficient circulation or respiratory distress is endangering the life of the patient, an escharotomy is a corrective procedure often used.

An escharotomy is an appropriate course of action when a limb is exhibiting loss of color, decreased pulse strength, diminishing capillary refill, and a changing neurologic status (progressive loss of light touch or pin-prick sensation) distal to the burn. [9] The procedure is indicated for eschar around the chest when the patient's respiratory efforts are compromised. Respiratory distress often will exhibit itself by short, shallow breaths or cyanosis around the lips. It is a good practice to complete the escharotomy prior to transport so that bleeding can be controlled and the wound dressed properly. [10] The need for an escharotomy can be reduced if the patient's burned extremity is elevated and constricting objects removed as soon as possible. [11]

When an escharotomy has been deemed necessary, the incision must extend completely through the burned tissue to ensure adequate release of vascular compression. [12] Incisions are generally carried out in the midlateral line of the burned limb. [13] [14] For circumferential burns of the chest, the incision is made along the anterior axillary line (Ill. 112). [15] Pain during the procedure should be minimal or even nonexistent, as the nerve endings in the eschar will have been burned away. The PHCP must remember to carry his incision through the eschar to the underlying connective tissue to allow for the desired expansion of the edematous tissue (Ills. 113 and 114) (Photo 80).

Illustration 112: Preferred sites for escharotomy incisions.

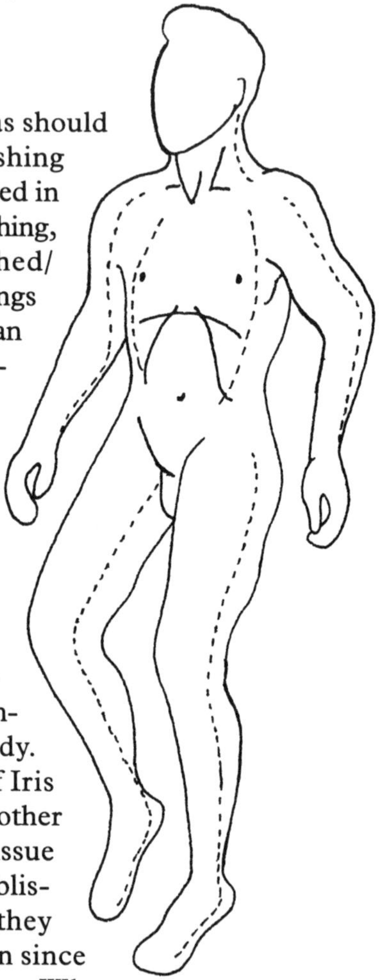

Cleaning and Debridement
of the Burn Wound

The cleaning of burned areas should be accomplished by gentle washing with Hibiclens or Betadine diluted in sterile saline or water. Bits of clothing, dirt, and loose tissue are flushed/scrubbed away. Adherent dressings applied as a first-aid procedure can be soaked off. During the cleaning of the burn, the solution should be at least room temperature to prevent the patient from becoming chilled. Every effort should be made to prevent the washing solution from running off one burn site into another. It is particularly important that runoff from burns to the buttocks is not allowed to contaminate other burns on the body. Along with cleansing, a pair of Iris scissors can be used to remove other contaminants and devitalized tissue that will not wash away. Intact blisters should be left alone until they break or show signs of infection since they protect underlying tissue. When infection develops within the blister, it should be opened and debrided (Ill. 115).

When cleaning and debriding the burn, the "no-touch" technique should be followed to help reduce the chances of infection. When using this technique, a "dirty" PHCP and "clean" PHCP are needed. With both PHCPs maintaining sterile technique (i.e., sterile instruments, gloves, etc.), the

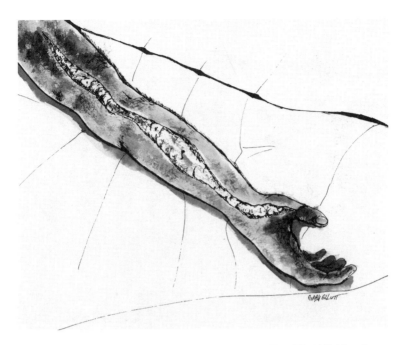

Illustration 113: Escharotomy performed on an arm and legs (Ill. 114). Note that the incisions have been carried over the joint and into the connective tissue. The swelling as a result of the burn has caused the incision edges to spread apart.

Illustration 114: This patient's feet did not suffer burns due to leather boots worn. Note site of venous cutdown in the right foot.

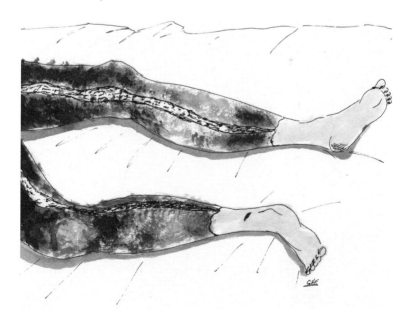

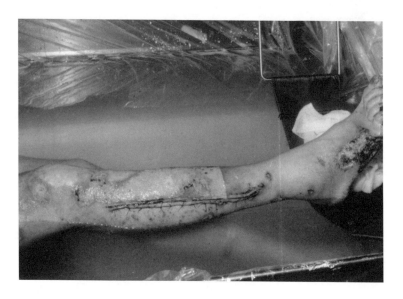

Photo 80: Escharotomy after having been sutured closed.

dirty PHCP is tasked with cleaning and debridement, and the clean PHCP is responsible for applying topical antibiotics and the dressing. The ungloved hands of the PHCPs should never come in contact with the burn site or the sterile instruments (e.g., forceps) used to apply creams and dressings. Once the patient has been dried off and a topical antibiotic applied, the wound is covered with a dressing (Photo 81).

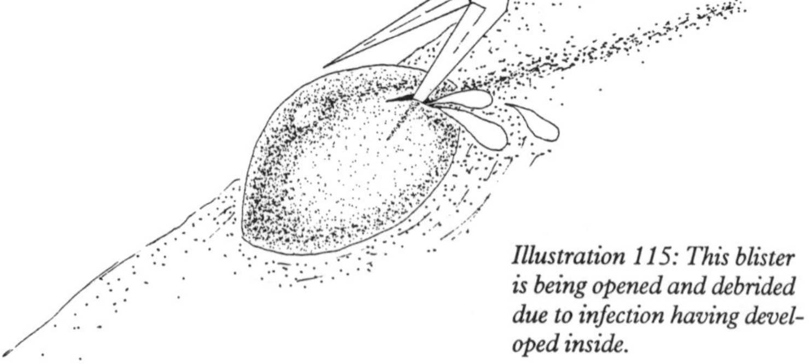

GHE

Illustration 115: This blister is being opened and debrided due to infection having developed inside.

Photo 81: Dressing of severe burns, with little equipment and less-than-sterile environment. (Photo courtesy of Rose Akers.)

White Phosphorus Burns

White phosphorus is a commonly used component of various munitions ranging from hand grenades to artillery rounds. It is generally used as an incendiary or an igniter for other munitions (e.g., ignition system of napalm bombs). [16] When the munition is exploded, the white phosphorus is exposed to the air, where it spontaneously ignites and is oxidized rapidly to phosphorus pentoxide. During the oxidation process, white phosphorus bursts into a yellow flame and produces a dense white smoke. These properties have led to its use as a screening smoke and in tracer bullets. White phosphorus will continue to burn until all of it is consumed or until it is deprived of oxygen. The regimen of care for the soldier who has suffered a white phosphorus burn is that of irrigation, neutralization, debridement, and dressing.

Irrigation: When the PHCP reaches the phosphorus-burned patient, he will be confronted with burns that are emitting a white smoke and garlic odor. [17] He should remove

the patient's clothing from the affected area. The burn is irrigated immediately with water to deprive the phosphorus of
oxygen and reduce the dissipation of heat into the tissues.
Given the limited quantities of water at hand in the field, wet
dressings may have to suffice.

Neutralization: Once the patient has been removed from
the combat area, attempts to neutralize the embedded phosphorus particles are begun by washing the burns with 1-per-
cent copper sulfate and 5-percent sodium bicarbonate solutions. [18] [19] The copper sulfate solution combines with the
phosphorus to form a blue-black cupric phosphide covering
that helps reduce further oxidation and enhances visualization of the phosphorus particles during debridement. The
copper sulfate solution should be applied for just a short time
and then rinsed off immediately to prevent copper toxicity.
The patient should never have copper-sulfate-soaked dressing placed on him. After the application of these solutions, the
PHCP must not overlook irrigation of the wound with water
or Normal Saline.

Debridement: White phosphorus will continue to burn
even when driven deep into tissue by an explosion. It is
imperative that all phosphorus particles are debrided from
the burn wound. This may be a near impossible task in a field
setting. When removing phosphorus particles from the
wound, metal forceps should be used since the phosphorus
may reignite (if not already burning) when it is exposed to
surrounding air. Once all of the visible blackened particles
(products of copper sulfate irrigation) and burning phosphorus have been removed, particles resting in deep tissue can be
found by locating the origins of the small columns of smoke
rising from the wound site.

Dressing the burn: Following debridement of the burn,
Silvadene Cream and a dressing are applied. The wound
should be inspected a couple of times during a 24-hour period to ensure that missed phosphorus particles have not
reignited. [20]

Final considerations for phosphorus burns: Given that

white phosphorus is used as a component of munitions, the PHCP may find his burned patient's wounds complicated by shell fragments. The phosphorus-burned patient may also suffer respiratory distress since the phosphorus pentoxide contained in the white smoke of burning phosphorus is a severe pulmonary irritant. As with all burns, IV fluid and antibiotic therapy should not be neglected. Phosphorus burns are generally considered more severe than other burns. They are known to heal more slowly and will in all cases be difficult to care for properly in the field.

A CASE STUDY
The patient, an 8-year-old boy from Zaire, received second- and third-degree burns on both feet while picking through a smoldering trash pile. The boy remained at home, where patient care was simply to scrape the burn with a piece of bamboo. After two weeks, the burn had become grossly infected, with extensive swelling and drainage. Local mission-

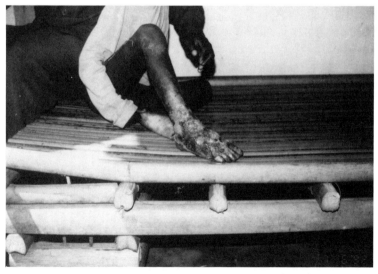

Photo 82: Grossly infected second- and third-degree burns with extensive swelling and drainage, as seen upon arrival to an aid station. (Photo courtesy of Rose Akers.)

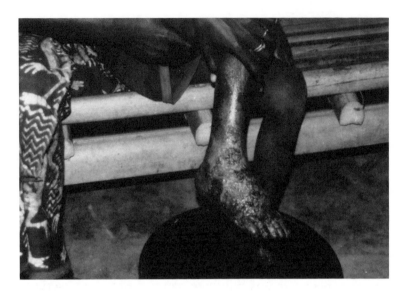

Photo 83: Betadine soak of the burn lasting 30 to 45 minutes. (Photo courtesy of Rose Akers.)

Photo 84: Burn on the fifth day of care showing signs of decreased swelling, although drainage is still present. (Photo courtesy of Rose Akers.)

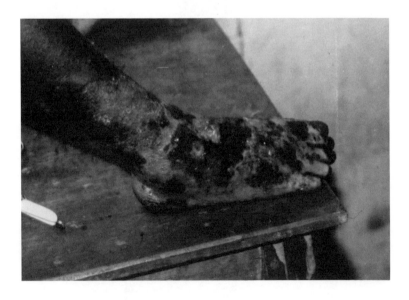

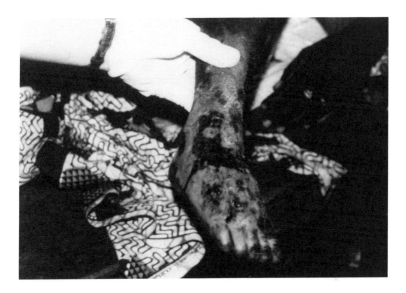

Photo 85: Burn on the seventh day of care showing much less swelling and drainage. Infection at this time is limited to a few small areas. (Photo courtesy of Rose Akers.)

aries began treatment for the patient with wound debridement, Betadine soaks, dressings with a topical antibiotic, and administration of oral antibiotics. On the ninth day of treatment, the burn had made significant enough improvement to allow the patient to return home. The burn eventually healed completely (Photos 82 through 85).

NOTES

[1] Yue Chang Heng, "Some Recent Progress of Burn Treatment in China," *Medical Corps International*, 1989, p. 18.

[2] *Combat and Survival* (Westport, CT: H.S. Stuttman, Inc., 1991), p. 922.

[3] Robert H. Demling and Cheryl LaLonde, *Burn Trauma* (New York, NY: Thieme Medical Publishers, Inc., 1989), p. 54.

[4] Thomas Clarke Kravis and Carmen Germaine Warner, *Emergency Medicine* (Rockville, MD: An Aspen Publication, 1983), p. 299.

[5] *Emergency War Surgery* (Fullerton, CA: S.E.A. Publications, 1982), p. 26.

[6] Thomas Clarke Kravis and Carmen Germaine Warner, *Emergency Medicine* (Rockville, MD: An Aspen Publication, 1983). p. 300.

[7] *Physician's Desk Reference* (Oradell, NJ : Medical Economics Company, Inc., 1982), p. 1151.

[8] Ibid. p. 1151.

[9] *Emergency War Surgery* (Fullerton, CA: S.E.A. Publications, 1982), p. 28.

[10] William G. Cioffi, Jr. and Basil A. Pruitt, Jr., "Aeromedical Transport of the Thermally Injured Patient," *Medical Corps International*, 1989, p. 25.

[11] Robert H. Demling and Cheryl LaLonde, *Burn Trauma* (New York, NY: Thieme Medical Publishers, Inc., 1989), p. 62.

[12] Ibid. p. 62.

[13] William G. Cioffi, Jr. and Basil A. Pruitt, Jr., "Aeromedical Transport of the Thermally Injured Patient," *Medical Corps International,* 1989, p. 25.

[14] *Emergency War Surgery,* (Fullerton, CA: S.E.A. Publications, 1982), p. 28.

[15] Ibid. pp. 28-29.

[16] Peter Reich and Victor W. Sidel, "Medical Intelligence Current Concepts: Napalm," *The New England Journal of Medicine,* 1967, p. 86.

[17] Thomas R. Konjoyan, "White Phosphorus Burns: Case Report and Literature Review," *Military Medicine,* 1983, p. 881.

[18] Theodor Kaufman, Yehuda Ullman, and Yaron Har-Shai, "Phosphorus Burns: A Practical Approach to Local Treatment," *JBCR,* 1988, p. 474.

[19] H.J. Klammer and J. Hein, "Burn Injuries—With Special Emphasis on Facial and Hand Burns," *Medical Corps International,* 1989, p. 12.

[20] Thomas R. Konjoyan, "White Phosphorus Burns: Case Report and Literature Review," *Military Medicine,* 1983, p. 881.

N[CHAPTER 10]UTRITION AND EMOTIONAL SUPPORT

After the PHCP has stabilized his patient and there is a respite from the battlefield, the focus of patient care must shift to a period of convalescence. Convalescence is an integral step in the progression toward total patient recovery. Of course the care of the wounded is modified by conditions and circumstances that govern the tactical situation at hand. A fluid tactical situation inevitably leads to a patient convalescing in an expedient base camp that is often primitive at best (Photo 86). Given such a backdrop, the PHCP's convalescent care of his patient may be limited to nutritional and emotional support.

NUTRITION

As the body begins to lay down a new framework of capillaries and tissue in the wound, it must be able to draw nutrients from the body. There is a direct correlation between the body's nutritional state and its ability to fight infection and generate new tissue. Troops in the field frequently consume insufficient calories, which, compounded by stress, has a detrimental impact on the body's regenerative powers (Photo 87). [1] If more than 2 percent of body weight is lost simply to sweat, both performance and recovery from physical activity can be affected. [2]

Photo 86: This temporary base camp depicts the environment in which the PHCP must be prepared to work. (Photo courtesy of D.E. Rossey.)

Photo 87: Joint American/MISURA team members just arriving back in Honduras after two weeks of operations inside Nicaragua. The emaciated, exhausted state of these troops is the result of extremely limited food rations during the offensive. Should these soldiers have suffered wounds, their normal healing powers would have been hampered. (Photo courtesy of D.E. Rossey.)

The PHCP must be diligent to maintain a balanced nutritional supply to the patient, whether this is via an oral or IV route. It may be necessary to add vitamins to the IV solution or feed a patient by a nasogastric tube. Patients should be encouraged to drink plenty of fluids (dependent upon their wounds), as studies have found that, when fluid intake is limited, field personnel will reduce food intake voluntarily. [3]

EMOTIONAL SUPPORT

Extreme behavioral and emotional reactions to the stress of battle have been recorded for as long as men have fought with one another. For the wounded soldier, stress mixed with despair can destroy his will to survive or alter his behavior so that he is unable to respond to the medical support given him (Photo 88).

Photo 88: American team member after having participated in extended operations inside Nicaragua. He is showing signs of physical fatigue, mental stress, and a lack of ability to function on the "local diet." (Photo courtesy of D.E. Rossey.)

To be of aid, the PHCP must establish communication with his patient, give an honest appraisal of the boundaries of help available, convey a sense that he is well in control, and, most importantly, generate the hope that there is a way out of this circumstance with confidence to know it can be done. Truth on the part of the PHCP is a defense against anxiety. There is no quicker way to set a patient emotionally adrift than for two separate PHCPs to answer a patient's questions with completely different responses.

The PHCP should remember that distraught patients can be left feeling very embarrassed after "unloading." The PHCP must at this time reinstill self-worth. Allowing the patient to participate in the decisions affecting him is a remedy for a tarnished self-image. This gives the patient a feeling of participation and an ability to cope.

Providing emotional support to a patient is probably more draining for the PHCP than the actual "blood up to the elbows" trauma case. The PHCP usually would much rather deal with the tangible aspects of emergency patient care. With continued exposure to trauma, the PHCP is capable of carrying out objective emergency patient care tasks in an automaton fashion. At the same time, he can relegate a potentially counterproductive emotional response to some little understood repository deep in the brain.

It is a special PHCP that can provide emotional strength and courage for both himself and his patients. It has been said that courage can be a consumable resource. If this is so, the combat-weary PHCP must learn to use his resources judiciously, as so many look to him for courage amongst the carnage of war.

NOTES

[1] John S.A. Edwards and Donald E. Roberts, "The Influence of a Calorie Supplement on the Consumption of the Meal, Ready-to-Eat in a Cold Environment," *Military Medicine*, 1991, p. 466.

[2] Madeleine S. Rose, Patricia C. Szlyk, Ralph P. Francesconi, Laurie S. Lester, and Robert Whang, "Acceptability and Effect of Carbohydrate Electrolyte Solutions on Electrolyte Homeostasis During Field Training," *Military Medicine*, 1991, p. 494.

[3] John S.A. Edwards and Donald E. Roberts, "The Influence of a Calorie Supplement on the Consumption of the Meal, Ready-to-Eat in a Cold Environment," *Military Medicine*, 1991, p. 470.

BIBLIOGRAPHY

Adriani, John. *Techniques and Procedures of Anesthesia.* Springfield, IL: Thomas Books, 1947.

Barnes, Steve. Personal Correspondence/October 1992.

Campbell, John Emory. *Basic Trauma Life Support.* Englewood Cliffs, NJ: Prentice-Hall, Inc., 1988.

Chirife, Jorge and Leon Herszage. "Sugar for Infected Wounds," *The Lancet.* July 1982.

Chirife, Jorge, Leon Herszage, Arabella Joseph, and Elisa S. Kohn. "In Vitro Study of Bacterial Growth Inhibition in Concentrated Sugar Solutions: Microbiological Basis for the Use of Sugar in Treating Infected Wounds," *Antimicrobial Agents and Chemotherapy.* May 1983.

Cioffi, William G. and Basil A. Pruitt. "Aeromedical Transport of the Thermally Injured Patient," *Medical Corps International.* March 1989.

Cole, Warren H. and Robert Elman. *Textbook of General Surgery.* New York, NY: Appleton-Century-Crofts, Inc., 1948.

Collins, Vincent J. *Principles of Anesthesiology.* Philadelphia, PA: Lea and Febiger Company, 1976.

Combat and Survival. Westport, CT: H.S. Stuttman, Inc., 1991.

Cooper, G.J. and J.M. Ryan. "Interaction of penetrating missiles with tissues: some common misapprehensions and implications for wound management," *British Journal of Surgery.* June 1990.

Cullen, Stuart C. and C. Philip Larson, Jr. *Essentials of Anesthetic Practice.* Chicago, IL: Year Book Medical Publishers, Inc., 1974.

Demling, Robert H. and Cheryl LaLonde. *Burn Trauma.* New York, NY: Thieme Medical Publishers, Inc., 1989.

Dripps, Robert D., James E. Echenhoff, and Leroy D. Vandam. *Introduction to Anesthesia: The Principles of Safe Practice.* Philadelphia, PA: W.B. Saunders Company, Inc., 1982.

Edwards, John S.A. and Donald E. Roberts. "The Influence of a Calorie Supplement on the Consumption of the Meal, Ready-to-Eat in a Cold Environment," *Military Medicine.* September 1991.

Eggertsen, Sam. "Teaching Venous Cutdown Techniques With Models," *The Journal of Family Practice.* June 1983.

Emergency War Surgery. Fullerton, CA: S.E.A. Publications, 1982.

Fisher, Daniel F., G. Patrick Clagett, Richard E. Fry, Theodore H. Humble, and William J. Fry. "One-stage versus two-stage amputation for wet gangrene of the lower extremity: A randomized study," *Journal of Vascular Surgery.* October 1988.

Good, Roger C. *Guide To Ambulatory Surgery*. New York, NY: Grune and Stratton Inc., 1982.

Grant, Harvey D., Robert H. Murray, Jr., and J. David Bergeron. *Emergency Care*. Englewood Cliffs, NJ: Prentice-Hall, Inc., 1989.

Grewe, Horst-Eberhard and Karl Kremer. *Atlas of Surgical Operation*. Philadelphia PA: W.B. Saunders Company, 1980.

Hafen, Brent Q. and Keith J. Karren. *Prehospital Emergency Care and Crisis Intervention*. Englewood, CO: Morton Publishing Company, 1983.

Hampton, Oscar P. *Surgery in World War II: Orthopedic Surgery, Mediterranean Theater of Operations*. Medical Department, United States Army, 1957.

Hardy, James D. *Rhoads Textbook of Surgery Principles and Practice*. Philadelphia, PA: J.B. Lippincott Company, Inc., 1977.

Heng, Yue Chang. "Some Recent Progress of Burn Treatment in China," *Medical Corps International*. March 1989.

Hell, Konrad. "Characteristics of the Ideal Antibiotic for Prevention of Wound Sepsis Among Military Forces in the Field," *Reviews of Infectious Diseases*. 1991.

Hill, George J. *Outpatient Surgery*. Philadelphia, PA: W.B. Saunders Company, Inc., 1988.

Jacob, Elliot and Jean Setterstrom. "Infection in War Wounds: Experience in Recent Military Conflicts and Future Considerations," *Military Medicine*. June 1989.

Kaufman, Theodor, Yehuda Ullman, and Yaron Har-Shai. "Phosphorus Burns: A Practical Approach to Local Treatment," *Journal of Burn Care and Rehabilitation*. May 1988.

Keegan, John and Richard Holmes. *Soldiers*. New York, NY: Viking, 1986.

Kessler, Henry H. "Amputation Lessons From The War," *American Journal of Surgery*. September 1947.

Klammer, H.J. and J. Hein. "Burn Injuries—With Special Emphasis on Facial and Hand Burns," *Medical Corps International*. March 1989.

Knutson, Richard A., Lloyd A. Merbitz, Maurice A. Creekmore, and H. Gene Snipes. "Use of Sugar and Povidone-Iodine to Enhance Wound Healing: Five Year's Experience," *Southern Medical Journal*. November 1981.

Konjoyan, Thomas R. "White Phosphorus Burns: Case Report and Literature Review," *Military Medicine*. November 1983.

Kravis, Thomas Clarke and Carmen Germaine Warner. *Emergency Medicine*. Rockville, MD: Aspen System Corporation, 1983.

Longnecker, David E. and Frank L. Murphy. *Dripps/Echenhoff/Vandam Introduction to Anesthesia*. Philadelphia, PA: W.B. Saunders Company, Inc., 1992.

Mattox, Kenneth L., Ernest Eugene Moore, and David V. Feliciano. *Trauma*. San Mateo, CA: Appleton and Lange, 1988.

Miller, Ronald D. *Anesthesia*. New York, NY: Churchill Livingstone, Inc., 1990.

Parke-Davis. *Ketalar*. (insert) Morris Plains, NJ. 1990.

Physician's Desk Reference. Oradell, NJ: Medical Economics Company, Inc., 1982.

Pories, Walter J. and Francis T. Thomas. *Office Surgery for Family Physicians*. Stoneham, MA: Butterworth Publishers, 1985.

Posner, Mitchell C. and Ernest E. Moore. "Distal Greater Saphenous Vein Cutdown—Technique of Choice For Rapid Volume Resuscitation," *The Journal of Emergency Medicine*. June 1985.

Reich, Peter and Victor W. Sidel. "Medical Intelligence Current Concepts: Napalm," *The New England Journal of Medicine*. July 1967.

Rose, Madeleine S., Patricia C. Szlyk, Ralph P. Francesconi, Laurie S. Lester, and Robert Whang. "Acceptability and Effect of Carbohydrate Electrolyte Solutions on Electrolyte Homeostasis During Field Training," *Military Medicine*. September 1991.

Serletti, Joseph C. "An Effective Method of Skin Traction in A-K Guillotine Amputation," *Clinical Orthopaedics and Related Research*. June 1981.

Speechley, Val. "Intravenous Cutdown," *Nursing Mirror*. May 1984.

Speed, J.S. and Hugh Smith. *Campbell's Operative Orthopedics*. St. Louis, MO: The C.V. Mosby Company, 1939.

Szerafin, Tamas, Miklos Vaszily, and Arpad Peterffy. "Granulated Sugar Treatment of Severe Mediastinitis After Open-Heart Surgery," *Scandinavian Journal of Thoracic and Cardiovascular Surgery*. 1991.

Tanner, A.G., E.R.T.C. Owen, and D.V. Seal. "Successful Treatment of Chronically Infected Wounds With Sugar Pastes," *European Journal of Clinical Microbiology and Infectious Disease*. 1988.

Textbook of Advanced Cardiac Life Support. American Heart Association, 1987.

Traverso, William L., Arthur Fleming, David E. Johnson, and B. Wongrukmitr. "Combat Casualties in Northern Thailand: Emphasis on Land Mine Injuries and Levels of Amputation," *Military Medicine.* October 1981.

U.S. Army Special Forces Medical Handbook. Boulder, CO: Paladin Press, 1982.

Westaby, Stephen. *Wound Care.* St. Louis, MO: The C.V. Mosby Company, 1986.

Wilber, M.C., L.V. Willett, Jr., and F. Buono. "Combat Amputees," *Clinical Orthopaedics and Related Research.* Jan./Feb. 1970.

Wolcott, Mark W. *Ferguson's Surgery of the Ambulatory Patient.* Philadelphia, PA: J.B. Lippincott Company, Inc., 1974.

Wolcott, Mark W. *Ambulatory Surgery and the Basics of Emergency Surgical Care.* Philadelphia, PA: J.B. Lippincott Company, Inc., 1981.